"Don't be mistaken. This book
your grandchildren. It's about l
parent, which is much better and far more powerful. It's what
makes this book so good."

Jack Klumpenhower, Author of *Show Them Jesus*

"As of this writing, I've been on this journey as a grandparent
for only a couple of years, but what a wonderful pilgrimage it is!
Truly 'Grandchildren are the crown of the aged' (Prov. 17:6). I am
grateful to have read *Grandparenting with Grace* so early in this
journey. But by the time most Christians become grandparents,
they have also started to give thought to finishing well as followers of Jesus. Larry McCall's book has given me greater biblical
clarity to the role godly grandparenting plays in that pursuit, and
has provided many practical tools for the process."

Donald S. Whitney, Professor of Biblical Spirituality
and Associate Dean at The Southern Baptist Theological
Seminary, Louisville, KY; author of *Spiritual Disciplines for
the Christian Life*, *Praying the Bible*, and *Family Worship*

"Grandparents who care about both their grandkids and the gospel
will find Larry McCall's book full of biblical principles and practical advice. Larry gets it: the important role that grandparents can
play in the spiritual development of their grandchildren, and the
scriptural mandate to do so is a message every Christian grandparent needs to hear and act upon. I strongly recommend that grandparents not only read—but study—*Grandparenting with Grace*!"

Larry Fowler, Founder of The Legacy Coalition

"Our grandchildren are gifts from God. With that gift, there is
an enormous responsibility for grandparents to help nurture
their grandchildren's love for the Lord and their spiritual growth.
Larry shows us how a gospel-centered lifestyle combined with
intentional prayer play a key role for grandparents. In this practical, Scripture-based book, you will gain tools to remember the
great purpose God has given you in this role and bless the generations that come after you."

Lillian Penner, Author of *Grandparenting with a Purpose:
Effective Ways to Pray for Your Grandchildren*; co-director for
the prayer ministry of Christian Grandparenting Network

"If you think being a 'good' grandparent is all there is to grand-parenting, Larry McCall will challenge that thinking in a convincing way. Well-written and engaging, *Grandparenting with Grace* will forever change how you view your role as a biblical grandparent. Larry's no-nonsense, biblical approach to grand-parenting—centered in the gospel, not culture or traditions—will transform you and your impact as a parent and grandparent. Filled with practical action steps, *Grandparenting with Grace* ought to be in every grandparent's toolbox for building a legacy worth outliving you generation to generation."

Cavin T. Harper, Founder and President, The Christian Grandparenting Network

"I found out my daughter was pregnant with our first grandchild a week before reading *Grandparenting with Grace*. I thought I was excited before, but after reading Larry McCall's book, my vision for grandparenting and excitement for my new role went off the charts. Larry has hit the sweet spot; he both inspires you in your role as a grandparent and gives you the practical steps you need to succeed. If you are a grandparent or soon will be, you should read this book."

Marty Machowski, Pastor; author of *The Gospel Story Bible*, *The Ology* (a theology book for children), *Long Story Short: Ten-Minute Devotions to Draw Your Family to God*, *Parenting First Aid*, and other gospel-rich resources for families and churches

"Being a grandparent is a wonderful privilege. It includes most of the joys of parenthood without some of the difficult challenges. Though multiple resources are available for parents seeking wisdom for godly parenting, advice for grandparents is practically nonexistent. This is a book every grandparent should read. It is refreshingly grounded in the gospel, essential for guidance in our relationships with our grandchildren, and is also filled with practical tips. If you are a grandparent, do not wait to profit from this invaluable resource."

Tom Julien, Former Executive Director of Encompass World Partners

"Our actions affect not only our personal lives but the lives of our children and grandchildren. It's a joy to live in light of the gospel, but it's an even greater joy to see the light of the gospel change those closest to you. Time and time again, Larry McCall writes and teaches with powerful and practical application. As a grandparent of thirteen, this is a book I have been waiting for!"
Byron Paulus, President, Life Action Ministries

"As an author and grandparent, Larry McCall has so many practical ideas and challenges for the parents of the parents. For all who get to love and provide fun and wisdom for their grandkids, *Grandparenting with Grace* offers insight ranging from the use of technology, ways to make memories together, and how to bless them in little but life-changing ways. Every mama and papa thinks about how their kids grow up so quickly. This manual of suggestions should be provided right away, every time a grandchild is born."
Knute Larson, Grandparent; pastoral coach

"I thank God for Larry McCall and for this book which inspires, challenges, and equips us with biblical vision and practical guidance for making known to our children's children 'the glorious deeds of the Lord and his might and the wonders he has done.'"
David Michael, Cofounder of Truth78 (formerly Children Desiring God); pastor for the Next Generations, College Park Church, Indianapolis

"Who would've imagined that a sound, systematic, and practical theology of *Grandparenting with Grace* would ever be available in print? Well, thankfully, Larry McCall has now written such an important manual for us! And, in doing so, has literally left no stone unturned in addressing this vital, yet neglected, area of Christian living. His over four decades of solid marriage and parenting experience (he has many children and grandchildren), along with almost four decades of faithful pastoral ministry, make this book a veritable source of grandparenting wisdom. This is an important tool for discipling your family until you see Jesus!"
Jerry Marcellino, Preaching Pastor of Audubon Drive Bible Church in Laurel, Mississippi; cofounder of FIRE (The Fellowship of Independent Reformed Evangelicals)

"Biblically-grounded, gospel-centered, thoughtful, practical, reflective, and intentional are just a few descriptions that come to mind when thinking about this outstanding new resource designed for grandparents who desire to serve their families and make a difference in the lives of their grandchildren. This well-designed book, which includes helpful questions and action steps at the conclusion of each chapter, will be beneficial for many, whether read individually or studied in a small group setting. It provides a wonderful reminder of the special calling and responsibilities that come with grandparenting, including the relationships with grandchildren and their parents, in both good times and in moments of challenge. Larry McCall is to be commended for putting together this most applicable volume."

David S. Dockery, President, Trinity International
University/Trinity Evangelical Divinity School

"This book is a must-read for grandparents. Every season of life could use gospel-centered counsel. With the grace of a pastor, the insight of a theologian, and the love of a gospel-filled grandparent, Larry has given us just that. Make sure you get an extra copy for your friends; they will love you for it and so will their grandchildren."

Louis C. Love, Jr., Pastor, New Life Fellowship Church,
Waukegan, IL

Grandparenting
with Grace

Grandparenting
with Grace
Living the Gospel
with the Next Generation

Larry E. McCall

New
Growth
Press
WWW.NEWGROWTHPRESS.COM

New Growth Press, Greensboro, NC 27401
newgrowthpress.com

Cover Design: Faceout Books, faceoutstudio.com
Interior Typesetting and E-book: Lisa Parnell, lparnell.com

ISBN 978-1-948130-69-1 (print)
ISBN 978-1-948130-79-0 (ebook)

Library of Congress Cataloging-in-Publication Data
Names: McCall, Larry E., author.
Title: Grandparenting with grace : living the Gospel with the next generation / Larry E. McCall.
Description: Greensboro : New Growth Press, 2019. | Description based on print version record and CIP data provided by publisher; resource not viewed.
Identifiers: LCCN 2019002165 (print) | LCCN 2019017057 (ebook) | ISBN 9781948130790 (ebook) | ISBN 9781948130691 (trade paper)
Subjects: LCSH: Grandparents—Religious life. | Grandparenting—Religious aspects—Christianity.
Classification: LCC BV4528.5 (ebook) | LCC BV4528.5 .M37 2019 (print) | DDC 248.8/45—dc23
LC record available at https://lccn.loc.gov/2019002165

Printed in the USA

28 27 26 25 24 23 22 21   4 5 6 7 8

DEDICATION

"Grandchildren are the crown of the aged," Proverbs 17:6.

What a delight you are to your grandmother and me,
Jackson, Katy, Kamaile, Titus, Ellie, Anna, and Josiah!
You are God's gift to us as your grandparents.
May we be instruments in the Redeemer's gracious,
sovereign hand in coming alongside your parents
in pointing you to Christ and his amazing gospel of grace.
We love each of you immensely!

Contents

Foreword

GRANDPARENTING WITH GRACE is a book about what matters most as grandparents—the salvation and spiritual growth of our children and grandchildren. Larry calls us, with a laser focus, to see and savor Christ and to allow the gospel to shape our grandparenting.

For many Christians, their understanding of the gospel is foggy and does not translate into everyday living. Christians understand that the gospel is important for salvation, but what about grandparenting? Everything in life, including grandparenting, should find its place in relation to the gospel.

God established the family as the primary means to evangelize and disciple the next generation. Parents and grandparents are gospel-partners, instructed by God to be disciple-makers of future generations. They share the same goal, but they have different roles. This book will help you rediscover the value of grandparenthood in the discipleship of grandchildren and ignite a passion to pass faith in Christ to future generations.

You will find that this is a Bible-saturated book. Larry McCall has written a book that is faithful to Scripture and grounded in the timeless truths of God's Word. That's why it's valuable. I'm delighted to see this book, because there are countless families, churches, and individuals who are in need of a renewed biblical understanding of grandparenting.

Grandparenting with Grace is an authentic book. Larry embodies what he writes about in this book. He walks the talk. Larry is a humble man, a faithful pastor, a husband worthy of imitation, and a loving father and grandfather. Larry seeks to live in a manner worthy of the gospel and can honestly say, "Imitate me as I imitate Christ" in this area of life. Larry would humbly admit he is not the perfect grandparent, but he is a seasoned guide and a godly teacher, and I can confidently commend this book to you.

Be careful with the book you hold in your hand. It may change your life and family forever. You will find that this book is a powerful call and a practical tool to help you take your responsibility as a grandparent seriously. Most importantly, this book reminds us that God designed grandparents to defend, display, and declare the gospel to future generations. May you be blessed by it and may the gospel shape your grandparenting.

Josh Mulvihill, PhD
Author, *Biblical Grandparenting*

Introduction:
What's So Great about Being a Grandparent?

SO, WHAT DO you think is the best part of being a grandparent? What's that well-worn quip? "The best thing about being a grandparent is that you can spoil the grandkids and then send them home to their parents!" Really? That's it? That's the *best* thing about being a grandparent? Hmmm . . . I hope not! Who wants spoiled children running around? There has got to be something better. So, what *is* the best part of being a grandparent?

I think for many of us grandparents, our enjoyment level is high. You know, "If I had realized having grandchildren would be this much fun, I would have had them first!" That's great. I'm glad you enjoy being a grandparent. My wife and I enjoy being grandparents too. Let's have fun with those grandkids. Let's keep our enjoyment level high.

But I wonder how high our understanding level is as grandparents. What I mean is, how much training have we received in seeking to understand God's calling on our lives as grandparents? How proactive have we been in exploring the Bible to find out what God calls us to do as Christian grandparents?

When my wife and I were asked to teach a class on gospel-centered grandparenting at our local church, we were taken a bit by surprise. It's not that we were against the idea. We just hadn't given it much thought. And I'm a pastor! We had done a fair amount of teaching on marriage over the years, and on parenting issues, too. But, grandparenting? Who ever heard of a class on grandparenting? No one had ever given *us* any systematic teaching on grandparenting. Yet, here we were, the grandparents of six amazing grandchildren, doing the best we knew how, even though we had never been given any training in this awesome ministry of grandparenting.

How about for you? Have you ever received any training in how to be an intentional, Christ-focused grandparent? Perhaps you are part of that small group of grandparents who have benefitted from one of the few Christian grandparenting conferences that have sprung up in recent years. I'm confident you consider yourself blessed if you have had that privilege. But for the majority of Christian grandparents, the opportunity to receive biblical training on grandparenting has not yet entered their radar.

Well, my wife and I said "yes" to the invitation to teach the class at our church on "Gospel-Centered Grandparenting." We knew we had a lot to learn. So, we began to search God's Word in earnest to understand his calling on our lives as grandparents.

We were pleased, but not totally surprised, when the great majority of grandparents in our church accepted our invitation to join us for our class on biblical grandparenting. Clearly, my wife Gladine and I were not alone in our desire to increase our understanding about this crucially important ministry.

I would guess that many of us approach grandparenting in response—either positively or negatively—to how we watched our parents be grandparents to our kids, or maybe how our grandparents interacted with us. We like how those who preceded us did their grandparenting, so we try to do the same. Or maybe we *don't* like the way our predecessors did their grandparenting, so we've determined to do it differently. And, to be frank, some of us haven't really given much thought at all to our grandparenting. Without thinking much about it, we've adopted the norms of our society, reinforced by the depictions we've seen of grandparents in the various media that flitter across our screens.

Maybe you are just now beginning this glorious journey of grandparenting, and the Lord has put in your heart a desire to know your destination before you set off. Or maybe you've been a grandparent for a while, and the Spirit is stirring within you a holy discontent. You no longer want to meekly go along with the flow of our culture's approach to grandparenting but, instead, to swim upstream in the direction laid out by our heavenly Father. You have a growing hunger to know more—to understand more fully God's calling in your life as a grandparent. You find yourself asking questions like, "Who are these grandchildren of mine?", "How does God want me to be intentionally involved in their lives for his glory?", and "Why does God want me to invest in my grandchildren's lives, anyway?" And in particular, "How does applying the gospel of Jesus Christ to the role of grandparenting actually work in real life—including some of those especially challenging situations today's families often face?"

Well, here you are, joining us on this quest to grow in our understanding of what God's Word says about our amazingly important ministry of grandparenting. Welcome! This is a book on grandparenting, but it's not primarily anecdotal. This is a guidebook—a book designed to serve grandparents by guiding them in how to apply the gospel of Jesus Christ to the ministry of grandparenting. My objective in writing this book is to take the glorious truths of the gospel and apply them very specifically and practically to the ministry of grandparenting. Paul wrote in Philippians 1:27, "Only let your manner of life be worthy of the gospel of Christ." The gospel truth is that we don't earn God's favor by our performance. Jesus Christ has already done that for us, on our behalf, through his life of perfect obedience, his death on the cross as our substitute, and his resurrection from the dead as living proof that everything he did sufficiently satisfied his Father's holy requirements. Standing on that gospel truth of all that Jesus is and has done for us, we can move forward in our Christian lives informed and empowered by God's grace. We have been called into God's family by his grace. Empowered by that grace, we can "walk in a manner worthy of the calling to which [we] have been called" (Ephesians 4:1).

So, how does that apply to the ministry of grandparenting? Well, that's what this book is about. As you read, my prayer for you is that you find greater clarity in God's call on your life as a grandparent and that you find hope and help by applying the gospel of Jesus Christ to those situations that arise in your quest to impact your grandchildren for the glory of our Lord.

At the end of each chapter I've included discussion questions and action steps to help you apply what you are learning, and deepen your understanding, so that the gospel can get greater traction in your daily life as a grandparent. Please don't skip these questions and action steps. In fact, maybe you would find it helpful to get together with some other grandparents in your church or circle of Christian friends. Going on this journey together would be a wonderful way to grow as grandparents who are centered on Christ and fueled by his gospel.

My prayer is that you will find the journey not only enjoyable, but truly helpful as you seek, by God's grace, to impact the next generation for life and eternity.

"Grandchildren are the crown of the aged"
(Proverbs 17:6).

Chapter 1

Learning about Grandchildren from God

The Blessing of Grandchildren

"HEY, BUDDY, COME on back in," I called to our nine-year-old grandson. He had just left my home office quietly, crestfallen after I had told him, "I don't have time right now." As he shuffled back into the room, I slid back my desk chair and pulled him close. "Do you know what the word 'irony' means?" I asked.

To be honest, the question was for me as much as for him. Our grandson had been looking forward to some time with me. Finished with school for the day, he had come bounding into my office asking, "Papa, want to play air hockey?"

"I don't have time right now," was my quick reply.

Thankfully, I was quickly convicted of the irony of how thoughtlessly I had turned down my grandson's request. The reason I felt I didn't have time for air hockey with my grandson was that I was trying to finish writing an article entitled, "The Best Part of Grandparenting!" After thirty seconds or so of trying to explain to this nine-year-old boy what an "irony" is and why I had asked, I abandoned the vocabulary lesson for some lightning-fast air hockey. He beat me, again.

That somewhat painful, somewhat amusing encounter with my grandson prompted some unanticipated self-evaluation. In what other situations had I communicated to him or to our other grandchildren that I was too busy to spend time with them? By my words, my demeanor, or my time commitments, had I given these young blessings the unintended message that they were, well, a bit of a burden?

The truth is, each of us struggles with self-absorption. That thoughtless "I'm too busy" response to my grandson led me to look, not only at my own life, but also at the lives of my grandparent peers. There has been a growing trend in American culture over the last couple of generations for the retired and semi-retired to devote the golden years largely to their own pursuits. The pull is strong in the hearts of many grandparents to move to "seniors only" retirement communities, perhaps in warmer climates, and to spend our time and money doing things we enjoy—golfing, shopping, cruising, eating out, whatever—with people in our own age group. The rationale is often, "Look, I've worked hard for a lot of years, spending my time and money on the family. Now it's time to enjoy myself!"

Adding to the decision to withdraw from regular intergenerational family involvement is the assumption we grandparents can easily make: "Hey, we don't want to interfere with how our kids are raising the grandchildren. So, we're going to enjoy life and make occasional fun visits to the grandkids, spoiling them for a little while, and then head back to our own lives. Anyway, being with the grandchildren can be pretty tiring! You don't want too much of a good thing, you know!"

Might not this sentiment reveal that many of us view grandchildren, not merely as a blessing, but as a burden we're not terribly interested in carrying? Spending snippets of time here and there having fun with the grandkids, spoiling them for a while, is fun. But intentionally deciding to give up self-pleasing pursuits so that we can pour our time and resources into the coming generations seems like a bit too much to ask. We love our grandkids. They are a blessing. But there is a limit, right?

But how does God see our grandchildren? And what does God have to say about the lives we might very much like to call our own? Is it possible we have missed something, that we've settled for a way of life in our "golden years" that fails to imagine the lasting impact God might want to make through us?

Jesus valued children. When his disciples wanted to preserve Jesus's time for more mature activity, Jesus "was indignant and said to them, 'Let the children come to me; do not hinder them, for to such belongs the kingdom of God'" (Mark 10:14).

And what do we read about the value of children in these passages?

- "Behold, children are a heritage from the Lord, the fruit of the womb a reward. Like arrows in the hand of a warrior are the children of one's youth. Blessed is the man who fills his quiver with them! He shall not be put to shame when he speaks with his enemies in the gate." (Psalm 127:3–5)
- "Your wife will be like a fruitful vine within your house; your children will be like olive shoots around your table. Behold, thus shall the man be blessed who fears the Lord." (Psalm 128:3–4)

God's Word clearly presents children as a blessing. Again and again, in both the Old Testament and the New Testament, we read of God's people placing high value on children.

7

"Grandchildren are the crown of the aged" (Proverbs 17:6). Even if that crown can feel a little heavy sometimes, God *wants* us to see our grandchildren as a blessing and live as if we really believe that!

Grandchildren as God's Special Creation

As grandparents, most of us feel that our grandchildren are "special." But why are they special? Is it because of their cuteness? Their special abilities, intellectually or athletically? Or is it just because they're "ours"? They may indeed be special in these ways. But as we think about who our grandchildren are in light of Scripture, we must acknowledge that their specialness comes ultimately from their relation to the Creator God. Like all human beings, our grandchildren are made in the image of God. The Lord clearly says in his Word, "So God created man in his own image, in the image of God he created him; male and female he created them" (Genesis 1:27).

Knowing that God made our grandchildren in his image impacts how we think of them and how we seek to guide them in life. Intentionally recalling that human beings—including our grandchildren—are God's special creations, God's image-bearers, gives us, literally, something of a God's-eye view as we go through life. Contrary to the dominant life perspective found in our culture, life is not to be lived from a merely human vantage point. Life is to be lived with the wisdom of God and from the perspective of eternity. And, by God's grace, godly wisdom and perspective often grow with us, as grandparents, as we age. It may be that we, as grandparents, are uniquely given by God to our grandchildren to provide the perspective and wisdom they will need to understand and live life well with their heavenly Father.

Because our grandchildren are image-bearers, they were created to be dependent on God, not only for life itself, but for how they *see* life—how they see themselves and everything around them. As God's image-bearers, our grandchildren should be guided to see that the answers to life's challenges are not found within themselves or within the consensus of the society around them. The answers to life's questions and challenges are found in God through his Word. Understanding this reality can have a direct impact on our grandparenting. Keeping this perspective will allow us to orient our grandchildren to a vertical perspective on themselves and their life by pointing them to God and his Word. "The fear of the LORD is the *beginning* of knowledge" (Proverbs 1:7, emphasis added).

As God's image-bearers, our grandchildren do not only reflect him; they are also accountable to him. This may be hard for some of us grandparents to hear, but our grandchildren are not the center of the universe. God is, and our grandchildren are in the process, like all of us, of learning to orient themselves to put away selfishness and immaturity. But sometimes in our affection and desire to give them good things, we can inadvertently hinder their spiritual growth, feeding their natural, but wrong, bent toward assuming that life is all about them. But wouldn't it be more loving to patiently teach and graciously model the truth that our life is all about God?

The very reason for our grandchildren's existence is to bring God glory (Isaiah 43:7). We have the privilege of lovingly guiding our grandchildren into a deeper knowledge of their relationship to God and helping them to make God-honoring decisions about their relationships and responsibilities as they walk through life. As more experienced followers of Christ, we grandparents are uniquely placed to come alongside these young image-bearers and train them to reflect on their lives with godly wisdom. We can bring God and his Word into our conversations with our grandchildren, helping them see how our lives matter to God, and how life is not a string of random choices made on impulse but has a God-defined purpose. We were made to reflect God in all we say and do. We were made to glorify God and enjoy him forever. That should be in the forefront of our minds as grandparents.

Yes, our grandchildren were made in God's image. But, there's something more we need to know about these young blessings in our lives. The reality is, our grandchildren were also made in our image. In the next chapter, we'll explore the Bible to see how it answers the question, "Do my grandchildren really need to be saved?"

Discussion Questions and Action Steps for Chapter 1

Discussion Questions:

1. What do you consider to be some of the blessings of being a grandparent?
2. What do you consider to be some of the challenges of being a grandparent?
3. How do you hope your grandparenting is different from your parenting?
4. What is one of your favorite memories of your own grandparents?
5. How do you hope to benefit from reading this book?

Action Steps:

1. Read Psalm 145 in a study Bible (The ESV Study Bible and NIV Study Bible are two of my favorites), reading the background notes, looking for truths about God that grandparents can pass along to their grandchildren.
2. Ask some of your friends who are also grandparents if they would join you in reading this book and discussing it together.

Chapter 2

My Grandchild Needs a Savior

YOU HAVE PROBABLY already noticed the sad reality that your grandchildren have minds of their own and want to go their own way, instead of God's way. Hopefully you and I have also recognized that tendency in ourselves. The prophet Isaiah put it this way, "All we like sheep have gone astray; we have turned—every one—to his own way" (Isaiah 53:6). That's a pretty good description of us all, grandparents, parents, and grandchildren: we all want our way and not God's way. That's what the Bible calls sin. And it's why all of us, grandchildren included, need a Savior.

Our grandchildren were born not only in *God's* image, but they were also born in *our* image. Genesis 5:3 teaches something about the human race in the wake of the sin of Adam. It says, "When Adam had lived 130 years, he fathered a son in his own likeness, after his image, and named him Seth." Did you catch that? "After *his* image." While Seth was born as God's image-bearer, he was also born in the image of his sinful human father. Seth was born a sinner and so were his kids, and their kids, and their kids—right down to you and me—right down to, yes, our grandchildren. King David's testimony is each of our testimonies: "Behold, I was brought forth in iniquity, and in sin did my mother conceive me" (Psalm 51:5).

This is not an isolated verse. You can trace the biblical teaching of our need for salvation all the way through the Bible (Genesis 8:21; Psalm 58:3; Proverbs 22:15; Romans 3:23; 5:12; and Ephesians 2:1–3). Because our grandchildren are sinners like us, just like us they need Jesus to save them.

How does accepting the idea that our grandchildren need saving shape our grandparenting? Understanding our grandchildren's need for salvation can help us to point them to their need for Jesus every day—for forgiveness and the power to follow him. Realizing that our grandchildren are sinners means that we won't give them the impression that they can make life work if they just try hard enough to live good lives while staying away from bad influences. It's true that our grandchildren were born into a sinful, fallen world infected by the sins of others and the curse that sin brought into the world (Genesis 3:17–19). Sadly, our grandchildren are and will be the victims of the sins of others. They experience the painful consequences of the sinful words and actions of other people—even those of their grandparents. This is one reason why we want to make repentance and forgiveness a reality we model in our family relationships. We also want to support our grandchildren's parents in protecting these young ones from unnecessary exposure to people and influences that can harm them physically, emotionally, and spiritually.

But the sin problems our grandchildren face in life are not merely external. Let's not say, "I've got wonderful grandkids. They're good kids. As long as we can keep them away from drugs, premarital sex, and other bad influences, they'll be just fine." No, our grandchildren's problems are not merely external. They need more than protection from bad influences. They need rescue internally; they need new hearts! God wants us to know that. He put that truth in his Book so that we would not teach our grandchildren that they are simply "good at heart." Although they are God's image-bearers, and do reflect his goodness, we want to teach them that they *really* do need new hearts. They, like us, *really* need Jesus. He said, "Those who are well have no need of a physician, but those who are sick. I came not to call the righteous, but sinners" (Mark 2:17).

God wants us to know that our grandchildren need saving—they need Jesus. This can motivate us as grandparents to passionately, faithfully pray for God to pour out his saving grace on our grandchildren while they are still young. Acknowledging that our precious grandchildren are in need of God's saving grace moves us to introduce our grandchildren to the gospel when we talk to them about the sin in their lives, when we read to them, when we pray with them, and when we encourage their families to be involved in a Christ-centered, Bible believing, grace-saturated church. Our heartfelt desire for our grandchildren is "that they should set their hope in God" (Psalm 78:7).

Isn't My Grandchild Already Good Enough for God?

Sometimes we grandparents struggle to embrace the thought that our grandchildren are in desperate need of the saving work of Christ in order to be accepted by God. It's so easy for us to default to, "Look, my grandchild is a good little girl. Why, I even call her 'my little angel'!" Of course, it's true that they really can be cute. They really are sweet at times. But they were still born with a sinful nature that needs the radical intervention of God's saving grace. The apostle John says it clearly: "Whoever has the Son has life; whoever does not have the Son of God does not have life" (1 John 5:12).

"But my grandchild is growing up in a Christian family and in the church," our hearts might protest. "Doesn't that count for *something* with God? Doesn't that give my grandchild an 'in' with God?" While we can be thankful if our grandchildren are growing up in a Christian family and are part of the Christian community, that doesn't guarantee their relationship with God.

Many of Jesus's contemporaries thought they had an automatic pass from God because of their parentage. They assumed that being born into the right family was their guaranteed ticket to heaven. But how did Jesus's forerunner, John the Baptist, respond to this prevalent assumption? "[D]o not presume to say to yourselves, 'We have Abraham as our father,' for I tell you, God is able from these stones to raise up children for Abraham" (Matthew 3:9). John the Baptist wasn't singing a solo on this issue. Jesus had a very similar response to people who presumed they automatically inherited a ticket to heaven due to their parentage (John 8:39–47), as did the apostle Paul (Romans 2:28–29).

If our grandchildren are going to be in a right relationship with God, being born physically into a Christian family isn't sufficient. They must be born spiritually into God's family. They must be "born again." The apostle John puts it this way, "But to all who did receive him, who believed in his name, he gave the right to become children of God, who were born, not of blood nor of the will of the flesh nor of the will of man, but of God" (John 1:12–13). Our grandchildren need to be saved from their sin by God's grace through the work of Jesus Christ.

How Do We Teach and Model the Gospel to Our Grandchildren?

In our conversations with our grandchildren, why would we hesitate to bring up the topic of their need for Christ? Might it be a fear of jeopardizing our relationship with them by pointing out their need for God's forgiveness? How much better for them to grow up experiencing their grandparents regularly speaking about God and our need for his saving grace. If our lives are characterized by dependence on the Lord and a continual celebration of the good news of the gospel, our grandchildren will grow up seeing that conversation about Jesus is a central part of Christian life. What if our grandchildren reached adulthood with many recollections of their grandparents verbally pointing out observations of God's astonishing kindness, listening to and singing songs about the glorious gospel, quoting or reading Bible verses about God's amazing grace, and thanking God in prayer for his undeserved mercy?

You know how strongly our memories are tied to certain aromas. Maybe you can recall a certain aroma when entering your own grandparent's home many years ago—possibly your grandma's cooking or baking. What aroma will your grandchildren recall years from now when reflecting on you? Wouldn't it be an inexpressible privilege if the "aroma" that came to their memory of us is that we "smelled like Jesus"? Oh, that we grandparents might be so saturated with Christ and his gospel that our grandchildren "smell" him when they are around us. "For we are the aroma of Christ" (2 Corinthians 2:15).

In addition to exposing our grandchildren to the aroma of Christ in how we live everyday life around them, we also want to be intentional in bringing to our grandchildren's minds and hearts their need of a relationship with God through his wonderful provision of salvation through his Son, Jesus Christ.

Look for age-appropriate books that are Christ exalting and gospel saturated that you can have in your home to read to the grandchildren or that you can give as gifts to your grandchildren who are old enough to read. Make sure that the books are not just telling children to "be a good little boy or girl," but are actually presenting the gospel. Before purchasing or borrowing a book to read to or give to your grandchildren, read it yourself. Is our need for God's gift of grace in Christ a focal point of the book? If you have skimmed through the book and have the distinct impression, "You know what? This book is presenting a Christ-less moralism," then it's probably best to keep looking for another option. It may be worth your time to read through some reviews of the book online or get input from a respected Christian friend or leader. Of course, having the books around your home unread has little value. So, if you have young grandchildren, why not plan to spend some time snuggled on your couch with them reading books that point them to Jesus? That's good intentional grandparenting. And as you close the book, use that precious time with the grandchildren to talk about God's grace and our need of him. Ask the young ones what questions or thoughts they have after reading that book with you. Share with them your own thoughts about what you just read together.

Similar counsel can be given in selecting other media, such as music and videos, that you want your grandchildren to benefit from when you're together. While there is nothing wrong with planning to watch a wholesome non-Christian movie with your grandkids now and then, why not be intentional in processing the movie with your grandkids in age-appropriate ways? What commendable virtues did they notice in the movie? What wrong attitudes or actions did they see? Were there any redemptive themes that reminded them of what Jesus has done for us? Also, are there some Christian movies that might inspire your grandchildren to live for God's glory? Take the time to research options online, or check out your church's library or even your local public library. You might be surprised to find that there are some great options available now that weren't available when you were raising your own kids. We have enjoyed introducing our grandkids to some Christian movies specifically produced for children that focus on the lives of missionaries and key leaders in church history. Afterward, we have taken some time to process the movie with them, asking questions such as "What did you especially like about this movie? Why is that?" or "What do you think God may want us to learn (or how might he want us to change) from watching this movie?"

When you are with your grandchildren, or interacting with them via the phone or social media, why not intentionally interact with them about what they are learning in Sunday school or in the worship service or in family devotions? With gentle enthusiasm, maybe ask something as simple as, "What was your Sunday school lesson about today?" then ask friendly follow-up questions, drawing out your grandchild's heart.

When you need to address your grandchild's sinful attitude, words, or actions, use your conversation to lovingly discuss the child's need for God's forgiveness. Don't thoughtlessly settle for moralistic exhortations along the line of "You need to be a better boy or girl!" or try to minimize their sin by saying something like, "You're usually such a good kid. I don't know why you're acting this way!" Instead of talking about your grandchild's "goodness," why not talk about the goodness and grace of Jesus Christ? We do take great delight in our grandchildren—and we tell them so. Let's also take great delight in Christ—and tell our grandchildren so. Let's intentionally give our grandchildren a gospel-saturated perspective. Let's talk about God, his Word, sin (including our own), and our need for God's forgiveness through Christ.

While we will discuss more fully later in the book the crucial subject of praying for our grandchildren, let's acknowledge here that it greatly benefits our grandchildren to hear us pray for them and with them. When we are with our grandchildren around the table or at bedtime, imagine the impact on the little ones' minds and hearts to hear Grandpa and Grandma praying for God to give them hearts that love and obey Jesus. If we're talking with our grandchildren on the phone, or sending them an email or text message, we can let them know not only that we're praying for them, but mention something specific that we're asking God to do in them or for them. If we're sending them a birthday card in the mail, why not add a sentence or two that mentions how we will be praying for them in this new year of life? Again, we want to intentionally seize opportunities to help our grandchildren think about God and our need for his grace in Jesus Christ.

And, most importantly, let's remember the power of reading God's Word with our grandchildren. Paul says in Romans 10:17, "So faith comes from hearing, and hearing through the word of Christ." And he also reminded Timothy that, "[F]rom childhood you have been acquainted with the sacred writings, which are able to make you wise for salvation through faith in Christ Jesus" (2 Timothy 3:15). When we are with our grandchildren, we can be intentional about reading the Bible with them. It might be just a verse or two that we read before bedtime or before a meal. At family holiday gatherings, we may want to plan ahead to read a holiday-specific passage. What a blessing for our grandchildren to grow up with the memory of Grandpa reading Luke 2 every Christmas or a resurrection passage at Easter or verses about giving thanks at the Thanksgiving family gathering. As grandchildren learn to read, enthusiastically involving them in the reading can keep them engaged. What an impression it can have on a child's heart to see Grandpa or Grandma reading the Bible in his or her devotional time, helping that grandchild see with his own eyes how much God's Word is treasured. Then, to watch his grandparent smile and hear him ask, "Want to hear what I've been reading this morning?" Memories can be made—possibly eternity-shaping memories.

What if a grandchild asks, "Grandpa (or Grandma), am I going to heaven?" Wouldn't that question make your grandparent heart skip a beat with joy? But how should we respond? What are some key issues to keep in mind in discussing salvation with our grandchildren?

First, it may be wise to gently clarify what prompted the question. Make eye contact and explore: "Why do you ask, sweetheart?" Does it seem like there has been a sincere stirring in his or her heart? Then, pray for God's guidance as you respond to your grandchild about this crucially important issue.

Second, use your Bible as you talk to your grandchild about how they can be sure they are going to heaven. Remember, "So faith comes from hearing, and hearing through the word of Christ" (Romans 10:17). Here are some key issues to draw from as you discuss salvation with your grandchild:

- God is holy. He made you and wants you to live your life for him, not just for yourself (Isaiah 43:7).
- But we *do* live for ourselves instead of for God, many times disobeying God just so we can get our own way. We often do what God says *not* to do, and we avoid doing what God says *to do* (Romans 3:10–12, 23). That's called "sin."
- Sin deserves punishment (Romans 6:23). The ultimate punishment is being sent away from the presence of God, into hell, forever.
- Jesus is the only person who never sinned (2 Corinthians 5:21; Hebrews 4:15). He always did what his heavenly Father wanted him to do (John 8:29).
- Not only did Jesus live a life of perfectly obeying God, but then he died on the cross to pay the penalty that we sinners earned for our disobedience (Romans 5:6–11). Jesus could pay our penalty because he didn't have to pay for his own sins.
- To be right with God, you must repent of your sin—you must turn away from it (Acts 2:38).
- You must put your trust in Jesus and what he did in his life and in his death on the cross as the only way you can ever be right with God (John 14:6; Acts 4:12)
- Ask him to forgive you and make you his child (Romans 10:9–13). Note: If the child wants to confess his or her sin and ask God to save him or her, I'd encourage the child to say that in his

own words. Sometimes well-meaning Christians assume that salvation is the direct result of praying "the sinner's prayer" and seek to get a child to repeat the words being offered by the adult "evangelizer," as if saying those words will somehow guarantee the child's salvation. But, we need to remember that salvation is a miracle of God's sovereign grace, not the mechanical result of saying certain words, even in a prayer. I wonder how many children have been given "assurance of salvation" by a well-meaning adult immediately after the child has prayed "the sinner's prayer." Is that really wise?

Sometimes grandparents ask me how they can know for sure if their grandchild is a Christian. And, of course, the answer is that only God knows another person's heart. Remember that the regeneration of a soul dead in sin is a miracle of grace—the work of the sovereign Spirit of God. Second Corinthians 4:6, "For God, who said, 'Let light shine out of darkness,' has shone in our hearts to give the light of the knowledge of the glory of God in the face of Jesus Christ." John 6:44 says, "No one can come to me unless the Father who sent me draws him." Salvation is not the "magical" result of saying certain words or praying a certain prayer or "asking Jesus into your heart." But you can always rejoice when you see the Spirit at work in their life. When your grandchild asks about salvation or heaven, rejoice that the Spirit is at work and point that out to them.

Remind your grandchild that becoming a Christian is as simple as turning to God and asking for forgiveness for Jesus's sake. Share God's promises, such as Romans 10:9, "[I]f you confess with your mouth that Jesus is Lord and believe in your heart that God raised him from the dead, you will be saved," and John 3:16, "For God so loved the world, that he gave his only Son, that whoever believes in him shall not perish but have eternal life."

If your grandchild has, while talking to you, asked the Lord to forgive him of his sins and asked God to make him his child, make sure you have a conversation with your grandchild's parents to tell them that wonderful news and discuss appropriate next steps in your grandchild's spiritual development. And rejoice in the privilege of encouraging this young believer on his or her journey of following Jesus!

Discussion Questions and Action Steps for Chapter 2

Discussion Questions:

1. When did you come to faith in Christ? Who told you the gospel?
2. What is it that our grandchildren need more than anything else? See Romans 3:23 and 5:12.
3. How would you explain the gospel to a six-year-old? What would you want to include in your conversation with the child?

Action Steps:

1. If you do not do so already, begin today to pray daily for your grandchildren to come to embrace the gospel, the good news of Jesus Christ.
2. Check out these resources that can help us understand how to explain the gospel to children: *Show Them Jesus*, by Jack Klumpenhower or the booklet *Leading Your Child to Christ*, by Marty Machowski.

Chapter 3

Developing God-Honoring Relationships with My Grandchildren's Parents

WHAT'S THAT OFT-REPEATED counsel to dads? "One of the best things you can do for your children is to love their mother." I wonder if we could tweak that advice for the realm of grandparenting. "One of the best things you can do for your grandchildren is to love their parents." After all, in the Lord's normal providence, no one has greater influence on your grandchildren than their parents. So, having a God-honoring relationship with your kids may bear a double blessing: the parents may be encouraged in their ministry of being their children's primary spiritual mentors, and the grandchildren may enjoy the fruit of parents who are more Christ-focused in their parenting due to the loving involvement of an older generation. Let's consider, how do we grandparents demonstrate our love and respect to the parents of our grandchildren?

Honoring Biblical Boundaries
Probably one of the most sensitive and potentially polarizing issues that grandparents face is determining what their role

should be in relationship to their grandchildren's parents—their own adult children and children-in-law.

Some grandparents, no doubt, intrude into realms that are the rightful responsibilities of the parents, bypassing the grandchildren's parents in areas of decisions and discipline. Grandparents who ignore or even openly defy generational boundaries often leave in their wake grandchildren who are confused about who to listen to as they seek to navigate their way through their developing lives. And the grandchildren aren't the only generation to be negatively affected by grandparents who have overstepped their bounds. What often happens to the grandchildren's parents when the grandparent wrongly usurps parental rights and responsibilities over the grandchildren? There are almost always negative repercussions. A common reaction from parents who are dealing with an overbearing grandparent is to look for ways to create distance. If polite attempts to explain generational boundaries have not had the desired result, the grandchildren's parents will begin doing what they can to limit the grandparent's involvement with and influence on the grandchildren. Visits and phone calls become briefer and less frequent. Overbearing grandparents increasingly find themselves left out of events in the grandchildren's lives and uninformed about extended family plans. And unless the grandparent humbly owns his fault in contributing to the stress that three generations are now suffering from, the family relationships will continue to become more stretched and strained.

But in some families, the parent responds very differently to the domineering grandparent. Rather than resisting the out-of-bounds grandparent with distance, some parents just passively go along, allowing the grandparent to assume responsibilities that parents should be carrying. These extended families with a domineering grandparent and passive parent often have dysfunctions that would benefit from the involvement of a Christian counselor. Is the parent living in fear of the overbearing grandparent, finding it easier to just go along than risk the potential pain of confrontation? Might a controlling grandparent be inadvertently enabling sinful choices in the life of the parent? The gospel can help these complex, broken families. If these sorts of patterns seem to describe your own family's intergenerational relationships, I encourage you to seek help from a competent Christian counselor. Denying or ignoring this brokenness might have long-lasting negative effects on your grandchildren.

Some grandparents have overstepped the bounds of what it means to be biblical grandparents, wrongly assuming a role in the grandchildren's lives that rightfully belongs to the parents. We might say that these grandparents have gone too far. But a much more common problem in our culture is the grandparent who has not gone far enough. Sadly, many Christian grandparents have not taken an active role in helping disciple their grandchildren in the ways of Christ because "that's the parents' responsibility." In saying that, the implication is that grandparents should deliberately leave the spiritual development of their grandchildren entirely to the parents. So, what's left for the grandparent to do? Well, many grandparents would respond this way: "I shouldn't get too involved in the spiritual side of things. I wouldn't want to overstep my bounds. That's the parents' responsibility. My role as a grandparent is to be my grandchildren's supporter—to be their friend and make their lives a bit more enjoyable and memorable. I want to have a fun time with my grandchildren when I'm with them—maybe even spoil them a bit—then send them home to their parents. The parents are supposed to be the ones to talk to the grandkids about God. I wouldn't want to get in the way."

But is that God's design for grandparents? Does God want grandparents to limit their grandparenting role to spending their time on fun activities and their money on gifts and trips?

There is clearly more to being a biblically minded grandparent without overstepping the roles and responsibilities God has given the grandchildren's parents. How might grandparents impact their grandchildren for the glory of God, nurturing them in the ways of Christ without encroaching on the roles and responsibilities that God has given to the grandchildren's parents?

Respecting Our Kids as God's Appointed Primary Spiritual Mentors of Our Grandchildren

Grandparents are not the *primary* spiritual mentors of the grandchildren. God has given that role to the parents. Ephesians 6:4 reminds us, "Fathers, do not provoke your children to anger, but bring them up in the discipline and instruction of the Lord."

How thankful we grandparents should be when we see our kids embracing the role that our Lord has given them, taking the initiative in discipling their own children in the ways of Christ. We give our own "amen" to the apostle John's testimony, "I have no greater joy than to hear that my children are walking in the truth" (3 John 4). We can and should regularly thank God that his grace is bearing fruit in our kids' lives as they seek to parent their own children in ways that honor Christ. We can and should take initiative in giving words of appreciation and encouragement to our kids, praising their faithfulness as the primary spiritual mentors in their children's lives.

But does the reality of the parents being the primary spiritual trainers of their children mean that we grandparents are relegated to the sidelines of our grandchildren's spiritual development? Clearly not. Deuteronomy 4:9 tells us, "Make them [the stories of the mighty things God has done for his people] known to your children *and your children's children*." That sounds like God wants us grandparents to be actively involved in the spiritual growth of our grandchildren, doesn't it? Remember what the apostle Paul reminded Timothy? "I am reminded of your sincere faith, a faith that dwelt first in your grandmother Lois and in your mother Eunice and now, I am sure, dwells in you as well" (2 Timothy 1:5). So, how are we grandparents to be involved in the spiritual lives of our grandchildren without usurping the role their parents have as their primary mentors? How might we grandparents honor God as we come alongside our kids in a significant, active, supporting role as they take the lead in shepherding their own kids in the ways of Christ?

Embracing Our Unique Role as Grandparents

Ideally, parents will *want* the grandparents' involvement in the lives of the grandchildren. Let's talk openly with our kids about their hopes and desires for us as their children's grandparents. How would they like us to come alongside in helping their children journey to God-honoring adulthood? What investment of time would they like to see from us? How would they like us to use holiday time? Are there gift-giving guidelines we should respect? How would they like us to handle situations requiring discipline? Taking an active role in listening to the wisdom, needs, and preferences of our children can help us respond with gospel-empowered humility and discernment, keeping the channels of communication open for further discussion when new situations arise. If we have ideas for our own involvement that our kids have not brought up, we can ask for their input in an open-handed way, continuing to reflect Christ-honoring humility.

But what if our kids do not welcome our efforts to come alongside them in supportive ways as they take the lead in raising their children? We still love our grandchildren, and we still have a role to play in God's plan for intergenerational relationships in our family. How might the gospel help us explore ways to open the channels of intergenerational communication and involvement without becoming pushy?

Applying the Gospel to Past Failures with Our Own Kids

Many grandparents would testify that the influence that they could have, and maybe even *should* have on their grandchildren seems restricted—either voluntarily or involuntarily—because of relational tensions with their own children. If you identify with this situation, might I ask you a personal question? Do you feel that your kids may be holding you at arm's length because you might have blown it with them as they were growing up? As many grandparents mature, taking more time to reflect back over their lives, they become more aware of their own earlier failures in raising their families—and we all do fail in various ways. If that's your own testimony, why not begin by humbly confessing to the Lord your own failures to consistently bring up your kids in a way that honored God? Ask his forgiveness for your failures in obeying his command to bring up your own children "in the discipline and instruction of the Lord" (Ephesians 6:4), and acknowledge his kindness in forgiving you because of Jesus Christ and the hope-fueling truth that, though you may have failed, Jesus did not fail in doing the will of his Father.

Then, have a heart-to-heart talk with your kids, honestly confessing your own failures as a parent. After expressing your failure, it would be good to specifically ask for their forgiveness. Tell your kids of your desire to be more intentional in encouraging and helping them and their children in the days ahead.

Before moving on, I should point out that some folks see the lack of spiritual interest in their adult kids and assume, "It must be my fault." Not necessarily. While we should not dismiss our personal responsibilities, neither should we own someone else's. It might be that, by God's grace, you *did* try to raise your kids in the ways of Christ, and they rejected your teaching when they reached adulthood. The fact is, however, that we may not know exactly why our children make the choices they do—whether due to our failures or something else. In view of the limitations of our knowledge, we would do well to cultivate a disposition of humility and sensitivity toward our adult children, seeking to become "quick to hear, slow to speak, slow to anger" (James 1:19).

Applying the Gospel in Building Growing Relationships

It can be scary to talk to your kids about your past failures and how that has contributed to currently strained or distant relationships with them and with your grandchildren. But the good news is that the gospel gives freedom. Since we are accepted by our Creator God, we are secure, because of the work of Jesus Christ on our behalf. And living in that security brings freedom—a sense of security in God's embrace—which can empower us to discuss our failures with our children and seek their forgiveness.

This security can allow you to humbly discuss with your kids ways they may have hurt you without becoming accusatory and demanding. You can explore with your adult kids how there could be healing and reconciliation in your relationship—a reconciliation that would honor God and benefit your grandchildren. Having prepared your own heart through humbly seeking God's help, you might ask your kids for a time to have an important conversation about your relationship with them. Mentioning your desire to have a Christ-honoring, mutually enjoyable relationship moving forward, you might express your feelings, that you believe there are obstacles inhibiting your closeness. Having confessed your own contribution to the strain in your family and having asked their forgiveness, you can ask their permission to discuss ways you have felt hurt by them. If they grant their readiness to talk about this problem, you can use language that is clear but kind, not accusatory or vindictive, praying inwardly for God to soften their hearts. You can express confidence in the Holy Spirit's power and willingness to heal your family. In the Lord's timing, perhaps they will listen, confessing their own contributions to the rift in your relationship, asking your forgiveness, and giving you the gospel privilege of being "kind to one another, tenderhearted, forgiving one another, as God in Christ forgave you" (Ephesians 4:32).

As you experience healing in your relationship with your adult kids, you can enjoy being more intentionally involved in their lives, even apart from grandparenting issues. Ask them about their work, heart concerns, hobbies, etc. Mark your calendar with their birthdays and anniversaries, sending cards that include thoughtful handwritten notes expressing your love, your appreciation, and your commitment to pray for them in the coming year. Make sure you are doing this not only for your own son or daughter, but your son-in-law or daughter-in-law, too. This might be challenging if you don't particularly *like* your child's spouse. But in God's providence, you have become family together. "Therefore welcome one another as Christ has welcomed you, for the glory of God" (Romans 15:7). Even if our relationship with our children or their spouses has had rocky moments, let us take the high road as mature believers, initiating love and acceptance and not waiting cross-armed for our children to first reach out to us.

Even if your kids live far away, it's not impossible to have a growing relationship with them. Don't rush through your conversations with your child or child-in-law when you call, anxiously getting through the polite preliminaries so that you can talk to your grandchild. Take some time to interact warmly: "Just wanted you to know that I love you. How can I be praying for you and your family this week?" Listen well, asking follow-up questions when appropriate. *Then* ask if you can talk to your grandchild!

Supporting Your Children by Teaching Your Grandchildren to Love and Respect Their Parents

"Children, obey your parents in the Lord, for this is right. 'Honor your father and mother' (this is the first commandment with a promise), 'that it may go well with you and that you may live long in the land.'" That's the Lord's directive through the apostle Paul in Ephesians 6:1–3.

One important way we can build a stronger relationship with our own kids is to intentionally help guide their children to honor and obey their parents. For example, if our grandchildren are at our home, and the parents have given directives such as restrictions on eating sweets or bedtime deadlines, why would we want to damage both our grandchildren and our relationship with their parents by failing to support and implement these guidelines? We may be tempted to wink at our grandchildren and quietly say, "It's okay. We just won't tell your mom and dad. This will be our little secret here at Grandpa and Grandma's house." But to do so is to quietly teach our grandchildren the lie that disobeying their parents is okay—even fun—as long as mom and dad don't find out. While this may make us feel close to our grandkids, it separates them (and us) from their parents, eroding bonds of trust that we ought to be helping to solidify. Surely, we don't want our grandchildren to learn to hide things from their parents! Perhaps, more importantly, we do not want to teach our grandchildren to dishonor the Lord by deliberately disobeying authorities he has put in place for their good. Wouldn't it be better to remind our grandchildren of their parents' rules, showing by our own words, actions, and demeanor that we respect their directives? If the grandchildren are struggling with obeying their parents' rules, we can listen to them, empathizing with the difficulty we all feel when we don't want to obey God or others, and quietly letting them understand we intend to respect their parents' rules. Colossians 3:20 makes an easy memory verse to work on together, even for younger children: "Children, obey your parents in everything, for this pleases the Lord." When our grandchildren *do* obey—especially when they do so with difficulty—recognizing and praising their obedience can be a profound way to demonstrate our awareness of the difficulty of being under authority and can help lay the groundwork for encouraging future obedience.

There may be times when, as the older generation, we genuinely disagree with certain decisions or lifestyle choices of our grandchildren's parents. While those concerns may move us to pray for our adult children's lives and even prompt us to have a private conversation with our adult children to share our concerns, we grandparents need to be careful to not demean or undermine the parents in the presence of their children. If a grandchild comes to us with questions or concerns over sinful actions or lifestyle choices in their parents' lives, it would be wise and gracious to listen carefully and compassionately, empathizing with our grandchild's feelings, then encourage our grandchild to tell God all about their concerns. In addition to teaching our grandchildren to turn to God when things are difficult, responding this way can help to reassure the grandchild that Grandpa or Grandma hears, understands, and cares.

Supporting your Grandchildren's Parents Through Words of Encouragement

Remember when you were a kid and one of your parents praised you for an accomplishment you achieved or a commendable character trait they noticed? Or maybe you don't remember such encouragement from your parents, but inwardly you ached to hear something positive from your mom or dad.

Even as adults, the parents of your grandchildren may enjoy some words of commendation or affirmation now and then. Words are powerful, aren't they? What's that biblical proverb? "Death and life are in the power of the tongue, and those who love it will eat its fruit" (Proverbs 18:21). Are our adult children hearing words of encouragement from us as they continue their own journey of parenting? Let's ask the Lord to give us a growing awareness of his work in the lives of our adult children. Then, when we see evidences of his grace in their own lives or in their family, let's go that extra step in thoughtfully recognizing what we see, perhaps pointing them to the Lord: "I just wanted you to know that I think what you're doing is great. God is helping you to _____."

Our words affirming God's work in their lives and their parenting may be used by the Holy Spirit to give some much-needed encouragement as they slog through the difficulties of family life. "Let no corrupting talk come out of your mouths, but only such as is good for building up, as fits the occasion, that it may give grace to those who hear" (Ephesians 4:29).

Discussion Questions and Action Steps for Chapter 3

Discussion Questions:

1. How would you describe your current relationship with your grandkids' parents?
2. Is your tendency as a grandparent to be "too involved" or "not involved enough" in your grandchildren's lives? Why?
3. How might you work more closely with your adult children in being involved in the spiritual development of your grandchildren?

4. What work might you have to do in examining your own history with your adult children? Is there sin you need to confess and repent of? What steps might you need to take to restore relationships with your children?

Action Steps:

1. Add to your calendar the birthdays and anniversaries of your adult kids and kids-in-law. What other special dates might you want to include as reminders to send a card, a personal note, or phone call in order to express your love and appreciation?

2. Plan a time when you can sit face-to-face with your grandchildren's parents in order to discuss with them how you can be more supportive of them as parents moving forward.

3. Make a sincere effort to reach out to your grandkids' other set(s) of grandparents in order to get to know them better.

Chapter 4

Intentional Grandparenting

What Does It Mean to Be Intentional as a Grandparent?

What comes to your mind when you think of the word "intentional"? What synonyms? Maybe "purposeful," or "deliberate," or "planned," or possibly "proactive." If there were a "grandparent intentionality spectrum," where do you think you would land? Perhaps on the left there may be grandparents who are not at all intentional in their grandparenting. Maybe they spend time now and then with their grandkids, but their involvement is mostly reactionary. These unintentional grandparents may respond positively when asked by their kids or grandkids to do something together, but they don't *initiate* time together; they don't *plan* their involvement with the grandchildren. There's no overarching goal to their grandparenting and no thoughtful steps planned on how to get there. In the middle of the spectrum, where many of us find ourselves, are the grandparents who are *somewhat* intentional. They occasionally reflect on their involvement with their grandchildren; sometimes they initiate doing activities together. That's great. But what would it take to move the needle on the "intentionality spectrum" further to the right?

Let's stop to evaluate. What is the overarching goal we have as grandparents? Is it to be our grandchildren's emotional supporters? Their cheerleaders as they move through their childhood and teen years? Is our goal to give our grandkids happy memories as they grow up?

Maybe we should tweak our question to "What is the overarching goal *God* has for us in our grandparenting?" What does God want us to be aiming at *ultimately* as grandparents? Consider the following passages (emphases added below):

- "Only take care, and keep your soul diligently, lest you forget the things that your eyes have seen, and lest they depart from your heart all the days of your life. *Make them known to your children and your children's children*" (Deuteronomy 4:9).
- "So even to old age and gray hairs, O God, do not forsake me, *until I proclaim your might to another generation*, your power to all those to come" (Psalm 71:18).
- "*We will . . . tell to the coming generation the glorious deeds of the* LORD, and his might, and the wonders that he has done . . . *so that they should set their hope in God and not forget the works of God*, but keep his commandments" (Psalm 78:4, 7).
- "*One generation shall commend your works to another* and shall declare your mighty acts" (Psalm 145:4).

In God's gracious providence, the torch of faith that was carried by those who preceded us has now been placed in our hands. God wants us to be faithful in passing that torch to the coming generations. The Lord is calling on us grandparents to be diligent—to be intentional—in showing our grandchildren the greatness and grace of our glorious Lord, so that they "should set their hope in God" (Psalm 78:7). Now, *there's* a worthy goal for our grandparenting: that at the end of our lives, our grandchildren will have "set their hope in God."

So, what has to happen for that to happen? We can gain a good perspective on what it takes to be intentional grandparents by remembering God's directive to the people of Israel. God's Word to the Israelites was to be intentionally passed on from one generation to the next. It was for "you and your son and your son's son" (Deuteronomy 6:2). And, how was God's truth to be passed from one generation to the next? That transfer of God's Word was not a one-time event. The passing of God's truth was to be an intentional, on-going commitment as one generation interacted with the coming generations in daily life. How does Deuteronomy 6:6–7 describe this intentional transfer of God's truth from one generation to the next? "And these words that I command you today shall be on your heart. You shall teach them diligently to your children, and shall talk of them when you sit in your house, and when you walk by the way, and when you lie down, and when you rise." It's a matter of intentionally making daily life interactions with our grandchildren into opportunities for passing along truths about God, how we are made right with him, and how we should live rightly with and for him.

Intentional Involvement in Our Grandchildren's Worlds

If we want to impact our grandchildren's lives in significant ways, we need to be intentional in building relationships with them that lead them to *want* to interact with us. To gain their love and respect, we must do what our Savior did: he entered our world and shared our life. We mirror his loving sacrifice by entering into our grandchildren's world and genuinely sharing their lives.

Our intentional venturing into the world of our grandchildren can start in their earliest days, even while they are babies and toddlers. We grandparents can make our homes not only a safe place for the grandbabies but a welcoming place. How encouraging it would be to our kids when they realize we've been intentional in preparing our home for the grandchildren's visit, in order to make their visit more inviting! While we don't have to go overboard, how much money and effort does it take for us to have in our homes some key baby items—maybe some diapers, a changing pad, a place for the baby to sleep, or an extra outfit for the baby after the inevitable spit-up or diaper leak? How about a rocking chair and some simple books that we can read while we rock that precious grandbaby to sleep?

As the grandchildren get a bit older, we can continue to be intentional in making our home a fun place for them, providing a place where they want to be—where they can make memories with their grandparents. Having some age-appropriate toys, table games, and outdoor activities can communicate to our grandchildren and their parents that we have been anticipating their visits and take delight in preparing for them. Even if finances are limited, we might take advantage of yard sales or the local thrift store, looking for items that our grandchildren can enjoy playing with when they come to visit. Or maybe you still have some of your own kids' favorite toys and games tucked away in an attic or closet. What fun to tell your grandchildren, "Your Daddy or Mommy loved to play with this!"

And, of course, as intentionally engaged grandparents, we don't want to automatically send the grandkids off *by themselves* to play so that we can continue our own preferred activities. As much as possible, we want to spend time *with* our grandkids. When we have that imaginary tea party, kick the ball around in the backyard, or make engine noises while we push the toy car around, we intentionally engage in our grandchildren's world, building warm relationships and making lasting memories.

And as the grandchildren move into their school-age years, we grandparents can be intentional in making sure we know when their various school and extra-curricular activities are scheduled. If possible, we can attend their athletic games, their musical or theatrical productions, or their school's open house. We can encourage our grandchildren by telling them ahead of time that we're looking forward to being there and then praising their involvement in the activity. Maybe we want to celebrate afterward by taking the family out for a special treat. Doing so might become a memorable tradition for your family.

Of course, due to distance, health, or work responsibilities, grandparents can't always attend their grandchildren's school or extra-curricular activities. But there are still ways to be intentionally engaged in our grandchildren's world, even if we can't be there physically. By putting our grandkids' scheduled activities on our calendars, we can make a phone call beforehand, asking the grandchild how he is feeling about his upcoming event, expressing our regrets that we can't be there, and maybe even praying for him over the phone. Maybe one of the parents could stream part of the event or send photos taken during the event, allowing you to make a follow-up audio or video call with your grandchild afterward to celebrate and encourage them. The key is intentionality—communicating to your grandchild by your words and actions that he is on your mind and in your heart.

Intentionally Inviting Our Grandchildren into Our World

"With." It's such a common, simple word, but it can denote such power—such potential. Think about Luke's observation in Acts 4:13, "Now when they saw the boldness of Peter and John, and perceived that they were uneducated, common men, they were astonished. And they recognized that they had been *with* Jesus." The religious leaders were amazed at the boldness of these common men and connected the dots that the power demonstrated in the lives of these former fishermen was due to their having been "with Jesus." Jesus had taken these men and the other apostles *with* him during his three years of public ministry, and by God's grace and the power of his Spirit, Jesus had "rubbed off" on them. They were changed men, having been *with* Jesus. Reflecting our Lord, we grandparents can invite our grandchildren to walk through life *with* us. We can invite them into our world, so that they can learn more about life and eternity.

Think of the possibilities. Though the primary responsibility for training and discipling the children is on the shoulders of the parents, we grandparents can come alongside and have life-changing influence on our grandchildren. What if we grandparents developed an intentional "with" approach to ordinary daily activities, deliberately including our grandchildren whenever possible, demonstrating for them and coaching them in helpful life skills? It might be as simple as coaching a preschooler on where to place the napkin as you are preparing the table for a family meal or teaching an older child how to bake cookies, fix a leaky faucet, or do the grocery shopping. Wouldn't it be helpful for a grandfather to teach his grandson how to shake hands when he meets an adult or to include him in putting gas in the car, teaching him some safety points in the process? I often intentionally wait to fix certain things around the house until one of our grandsons, who is a hands-on learner, is present, encouraging him to help me think through how to fix that broken item. And, as the children grow, their ability to engage in daily responsibilities and chores grows, too. Helping our grandchild learn how to ride a bike has morphed (overnight, it seems!) into helping her learn how to drive a car. However we do it, we can assist our adult children in the amazing responsibility of preparing our grandchildren for life by doing life *with* our grandchildren. This mind-set can provide increased opportunities to impact their lives for God's glory, helping shape them for life and eternity.

Intentionally Pursuing Adventures with Our Grandchildren

If our heartfelt, prayerful desire for our grandchildren is that they become fully devoted followers of Jesus Christ, why would we encourage them to "play it safe" or to pursue a life-style of ease and comfort? Life is not centered on us. Life is centered on Jesus Christ, and following him is costly. What did Jesus say? "If anyone would come after me, let him deny himself and take up his cross daily and follow me. For whoever would save his life will lose it, but whoever loses his life for my sake will save it" (Luke 9:23–24).

Without being unnecessarily harsh, we grandparents can inspire our grandchildren to "do hard things for God." The pioneer Reformed Baptist missionary to India, William Carey, is widely quoted as saying, "Expect great things from God; attempt great things for God." What might be some things we grandparents can do to influence our grandchildren to "attempt great things for God" over the course of their lifetimes?

Clearly, we must pray, and pray for more than our grandchildren's safety and comfort in life. We want to intentionally pray that the Spirit of God will move in their hearts in such a way that they will want to be "all in" for Christ and the spread of his gospel. We also can model a lifestyle that shows that *our* ultimate goal in life is not our own comfort or safety but the spread of the glory of Christ in the world. This commitment in our lives will be evident, not only by what we talk about, but by how we use our time, our money, and our things. Do our grandchildren see us using the bulk of our time pursuing our favorite activities, or do they see us investing a significant portion of our time serving our local church or helping in a local ministry, such as a homeless shelter, a community garden, or a crisis pregnancy center? Do they see Grandpa and Grandma indulging themselves with their money, or do they see us investing in God's kingdom through sacrificial giving? Do our grandchildren see us being protective of our possessions, unwilling to let others use our stuff for fear of it being damaged or stolen, or do they see us mirroring Christ's generosity by gladly lending our things and opening up our home in gracious hospitality? Our grandchildren are watching us. What do they see?

Being intentional about attempting great things for God might begin right where you are. Maybe as a grandparent you discuss with your grandchildren something you could do together to serve their parents in some unexpected way, like cleaning their car or mowing the lawn or weeding the flower bed. Maybe you could work together to prepare a meal and deliver it to someone in the church or neighborhood who is sick, or serve together at a soup kitchen or homeless shelter. Talk to your grandchildren about their friends and family members who need Christ, and then join them in praying for the salvation for the people they care about. Design a bulletin board in your home to post missionary prayer cards, then pray together for those missionaries. As the grandchildren get a bit older, consider going together on a missions trip if you are able. If you take a big step like this, you could explore with your grandchildren how they might earn or raise funds for the costs of the mission trip.

As we age, it can be so tempting to focus on comfort and safety—for ourselves and for our grandchildren. Our tendency can be to make the safety of our grandchildren one of our chief concerns. Understandably, we encourage our grandchildren not to foolishly do dangerous things. Yet we need to face the possibility that we have leaned too far in the direction of safety and comfort. Doesn't living for Jesus involve taking risks?

Doesn't it involve personal sacrifice? As grandparents, let's do some honest evaluation of the example we're setting for our grandchildren—of the impact our words might be having on them. It would be glorious if our grandchildren would grow up with memories of grandparents who intentionally communicated by *example* as well as by counsel: Let's live radically for Jesus. He is worth it!

Intentionally Engage Your Grandchildren in Meaningful Conversation

What do we tend to talk about with our grandchildren? I'm sure a lot depends on the situation and current age of our grandchildren. But, no matter if our grandchild is eight or eighteen, are the majority of our conversations meaningful? Are we thoughtfully processing life with our grandchildren in our verbal interaction with them, whether those conversations are happening face to face, on the phone, or through social media?

I wonder how much we could improve our conversations with our grandchildren through the simple step of intentionally asking more open questions—significant questions. For example, instead of asking our grandchild a "closed" question (one that can be answered with a simple "yes" or "no"), such as "Hey, buddy, did you enjoy school today?" we could ask a more significant "open" question such as, "So, what would you say was the biggest challenge you faced at school today?" The answer to that question could open up all kinds of opportunities to *lean in to our grandkids' world*, to explore their concerns, to offer comfort, to encourage them, and to explore ways the gospel might relate to their situations.

Let's look for opportunities to engage in meaningful conversations with our grandchildren. It might be a significant birthday, such as becoming a teenager or turning eighteen. It might be when a child starts going to school, or enters high school, or graduates. What sorts of questions would you want to explore with your grandchild at those milestones?

Having these kinds of conversations with our grandchildren might require growth in our own patterns of how we relate to others. I know I am still in the process of learning to be less self-focused, more curious about others, and a better listener. We can change. We can grow. If we are true followers of Jesus Christ, we have the Holy Spirit in our lives. He can and does change us. So, why don't we ask him, "Please, Lord, help me be less focused on myself, and to 'Do nothing from selfish ambition or conceit, but in humility count others more significant than myself'" (Philippians 2:3).

As we grow in Christ-like regard for others, we can intentionally initiate conversations with our grandchildren on spiritually significant issues. For example, we might ask a grandchild, "What did you learn in Sunday school (or in youth group or from the pastor's sermon)?" Maybe we then explore that passage or topic with the child for a few minutes, looking for its meaning and impact on the child's life. Or perhaps we can welcome our grandchild into our own spiritual life: "Guess what I was reading in my Bible this morning. I was reading (fill in the blank), and do you know what that got me thinking about?" And the conversation develops, so it is not only about the words on the page, but about the impact of God's Word on your life personally. Discussing the Bible personally with our grandchildren demonstrates for them its power in our own lives. When grandchildren are old enough to read, we can encourage them to read the Bible on their own or with us. Having conversations together about Scripture can allow us to process what they're reading, asking them how a passage impacted them or what questions it stirred.

When our grandchildren are struggling with their own sin or the pain of being sinned against, we can process that pain and confusion with them. We don't serve our grandchildren by minimizing their pain. Instead, let's listen to their pain and struggles. This might mean gently asking questions, being quiet with them, or even crying with them. And it will mean going to God's throne room with them in prayer. We grandparents can be a "safe place" for our grandchildren to talk openly about their questions, struggles, and hurts. Let's determine ahead of time that, by God's grace, we will humbly and lovingly engage them where they are. Your grandchild may be facing a painful time in his life that you need to process with him—the death of a friend or family member, moving to a new community, or the separation of his parents. We may feel at a loss to know what to say, but let's ask the Lord to fill us with his Spirit and give us the wisdom and sensitivity to be present and to know what to say and what not to say.

Intentionally Affirming Our Grandchildren

Do our grandchildren know we love them—really love them? We have so many ways we can intentionally affirm our grandchildren and reassure them of our love. Nothing beats just coming out and saying the words, "I love you, buddy" or "I love you, sweetheart." Some of us grew up never hearing those sweet words from our own grandparents or parents. But, by God's empowering grace, we can reflect his love for us by regularly verbalizing to our grandchildren, "I love you!"

We can demonstrate our love for our grandchildren through appropriate affection—hugs and kisses. Again, if you grew up not being shown proper physical affection, showing affection to your own family members might feel awkward. But isn't it worth overcoming our hesitations for the sake of letting our grandchildren (and children) know how much we love them?

Intentionally affirming our grandchildren through appropriate words of praise can make an impact as well. We can ask the Lord to make us more observant of his gifts of kindness and grace to our grandchildren, then intentionally point those out to them. The praise we give should not ignore God's involvement, but instead, draw attention to him. For example, if you have an academically gifted grandchild, it would be so easy to brag, "You sure are smart!" But, how much more meaningful to say, "You know, it seems that God has given you an unusual ability to learn. I'm praying that you will use that ability to serve God and to bless others." Similar things might be said to a grandchild who has accomplished something notable in athletics or art or music. How encouraging might it be for a grandparent to affirm a grandson or granddaughter who has gone above and beyond the call of duty in serving others or in showing compassion to a hurting sibling or friend. Let's intentionally look for those evidences of God's grace to our grandchild or through our grandchild, then point out that virtue or ability in a way that honors the God who enabled that blessing.

Thankfully, there is a growing movement in the realm of Christian grandparenting for grandparents to be intentional in speaking words of blessing on grandchildren. These might be planned comments on a child's birthday or premeditated words spoken over each grandchild at family gatherings such as Thanksgiving or Christmas. What words of blessing might a grandfather or grandmother say over each grandchild, affirming God's goodness for that particular child and offering a personal prayer for each individual grandchild?

Discussion Questions and Actions Steps for Chapter 4

Discussion Questions:

1. How did your own grandparents intentionally engage (or not engage) in your life? If you had an intentional grandparent, what was it about him or her that made you feel that he or she was intentionally focused on you?

2. What memories or traditions are you intentionally hoping to leave with your grandchildren? How do you pursue making those memories?

3. As you reflect back over this chapter, what are some practical changes you could make in the next month to be more intentionally engaged with your grandchildren?

4. What activities are currently taking time that you could be pouring into your relationship with your grandchildren? What needs to happen to help you shift how you use your time for the benefit of your grandchildren?

Action Steps:

1. If you've not done so already, how about putting each of your grandchildren's birthdays on your calendar? Don't forget to check "repeat annually," and indicate that you want a timely reminder so that you will have an opportunity to write a thoughtful note of encouragement. What other special events for your grandchildren should you put on your calendar?

2. Write out a "blessing" to speak over each of your grandchildren on a special occasion in the coming year—possibly on their birthdays or at a family gathering such as Thanksgiving. If you are not able to be physically present with a grandchild on that special day, why not place a video call for that purpose? Or you could print out your blessing and give a copy to the child and his or her parents.

3. Schedule an "adventure" with your grandchildren for the coming year. This might involve going on a trip together, doing a project for someone in need, serving together in your church or at a local ministry, or just camping in the backyard. Plan the adventure with your grandkids, getting their input on what would make it special. Talk afterward

about what you learned or accomplished during your shared adventure.

4. Pick a verse or short passage you can memorize with your grandchildren. Make sure the length is appropriate for your grandchild's level of development. Make it fun, laughing with them when you goof up!

Chapter 5

The Power of a Praying Grandparent

"The prayer of a righteous [grandparent]
has great power as it is working."
(James 5:16, adapted by author).

Praying for Ourselves as Grandparents

What's the refrain of that old spiritual? *"It's me, it's me, O Lord, standing in the need of prayer. It's me, it's me, O Lord, standing in the need of prayer."* It's true, isn't it? While grandparenting those precious grandkids of ours is an amazing privilege, it's also a sobering responsibility. The life examples we are setting and the interactions we are having with our grandchildren can have a huge impact on the coming generation for good or for ill. When we pause to reflect on that reality, don't we feel the need for God's help? So, how do we pray for ourselves and our ministry of grandparenting?

Let's pray for our hearts. What beliefs and motivations do we hold within our hearts that shape our approach to grandparenting? If our core motivation, for example, is that we just want our grandkids to be happy, then our grandparenting will be given over largely to spending our time and money to make sure our grandchildren are having a good time. But, doesn't God want us grandparents to have objectives that go deeper and further than that? Remember the commission that God gave parents and grandparents in Psalm 78:5–7? "He established a testimony in Jacob and appointed a law in Israel, which he commanded our fathers to teach to their children, that the next generation might know them, the children yet unborn, and arise and tell them to their children, *so that they should set their hope in God*" (emphasis added). Are we grandparents approaching our ministry of grandparenting with that God-given priority burning in our hearts? Let's ask God to stir our hearts so that our motivations resonate with his.

Let's pray also for our understanding. It's hard to teach our grandchildren something we don't know ourselves! Maybe we should echo King David's prayer: "Make me to know your ways, O LORD; teach me your paths. Lead me in your truth and teach me, for you are the God of my salvation" (Psalm 25:4–5). As we continue to grow day by day in our understanding of God's Word, we ourselves will grow in faithfulness as his disciples and will have a treasury of wisdom and godliness to share with our grandchildren, helping them to trust and obey God.

Let's pray for wisdom. As grandchildren continue to grow, seeking to find their way through this often confusing, fallen world we live in, they will sometimes look to us for direction. How do we know what to say and what not to say? How do we know when to intervene and when not to intervene? How do we know what tone of voice to use in various situations? Grandparenting can be such a weighty responsibility. Maybe we should adapt King Solomon's prayer, making it our own: "Give your servant therefore an understanding mind to govern your people [to help shepherd these grandchildren], that I may discern between good and evil" (1 Kings 3:9). If that is your prayer, be assured, "If any of you lacks wisdom, let him ask God, who gives generously to all without reproach, and it will be given him" (James 1:5). Isn't that good news?

Let's pray for consistency in the example we set for our grandchildren as we point them to Christ. *Nothing* turns off a young person more quickly than the hypocritical life of someone in authority over them. Our grandkids (and our adult children) will quickly lose interest if we are saying one thing with our lips and another thing with our lives. We need to ask the Lord to keep us close on the heels of Jesus as we live day by day, so that we can say to our grandchildren with integrity, "Be imitators of me, as I am of Christ" (1 Corinthians 11:1).

Let's pray for perseverance in our prayers for our grandchildren. Pray that we don't give up when we don't see immediate answers to our prayers. Some prayers might not be answered in our lifetimes, but maybe we'll find out in eternity how God answered those passionate requests. "Pray without ceasing" (1 Thessalonians 5:17).

And let's pray for strength! With each additional candle on our birthday cakes, we feel an increased need for energy, don't we? This prayer can seem very relevant after some hours with our very active grandchildren: "Do not cast me off in the time of old age; forsake me not when my strength is spent" (Psalm 71:9). Amen and amen!

Praying for Our Grandchildren's Parents

In the Lord's normal providence, no one will have a greater impact on our grandchildren than their own parents—our kids and kids-in-law. They are God's designated "primary disciple makers" in the lives of our grandchildren. So, how should we pray for our grandchildren's parents?

Are any of your kids or kids-in-law still without saving faith in Christ? Praying for their salvation is clearly a priority. Don't our hearts resonate when we read in Romans 10:1 the apostle Paul's concern for his own Jewish kinfolk, "Brothers, my heart's desire and prayer to God for them is that they may be saved"? In the same way, let's go to our gracious, sovereign

Father, asking him to put his amazing grace on display in saving our adult children. "Lord, give my son or daughter eyes to see 'the light of the knowledge of the glory of God in the face of Jesus Christ' (2 Corinthians 4:6). Please, give him or her ears to hear the precious voice of the Good Shepherd (John 10:3). Will you apply to my son or daughter your promise, 'I will give you a new heart, and a new spirit I will put within you. And I will remove the heart of stone from your flesh and give you a heart of flesh' (Ezekiel 36:26)?"

Let's pray that our adult children would grow in grace. How might Colossians 2:6–7 be turned into a prayer for our kids? Paul writes, "[A]s you received Christ Jesus the Lord, so walk in him, rooted and built up in him and established in the faith, just as you were taught, abounding in thanksgiving." Perhaps, "Lord, thank you for blessing our kids with the gift of salvation. Now, Lord, would you help him or her grow in that same grace, increasing in gratitude as they realize more fully their security and purpose in Christ?" Let's remember to pray that our adult kids would make time to read God's Word, soaking in the wonders of God, seeing applications of his gospel to their everyday lives as individuals, in their marriages, and in their parenting. We can ask the Lord to keep our adult children strongly connected to a Bible-teaching, Christ-centered local church so that they can grow in grace and serve in ways that bring God glory. And let's pray that they would live lives that provide an inviting example to our grandkids of what it means to walk through life in a manner worthy of the gospel (Ephesians 4:1).

What Christian graces come to your mind as being especially desirable or necessary when you reflect on your own years of rearing children? Wisdom? Faith? Love? Compassion? Humility? We needed these gifts from God when we were raising our own kids, didn't we? Well, no doubt our kids need the same grace as they navigate their way through the challenging years of raising a family. Let's pray for our adult children accordingly, asking God to supply what they need and to help them to rely on his daily grace.

A specific prayer request that comes to my mind concerns our sons and sons-in-law. Sadly, in our contemporary American culture, few men have been discipled in how to be God-honoring, Christ-reflecting husbands and fathers. Some men veer too far in one direction as they seek to lead their families. They become harsh and even abusive in their words and demeanor. Other men go toward the opposite end of the spectrum and become passive. They don't know how to lead and love, so they hardly try. Their wives are hurting, and their children are confused as they look to the man of the family to lovingly lead but do not get much direction. As the older generation, let's not ignore this prevalent problem in our extended family. Let's go to the Lord, asking him to work in the lives of our sons and sons-in-law, giving the humility to acknowledge their need for help and the courage to go look for it. Let's pray for God to give them godly mentors, realizing that we grandfathers may be the answer to our own prayers.

Praying for Our Grandchildren

Let's pause and consider the typical content of our prayers for our grandchildren. What tend to be the dominant concerns we bring before the Lord when we pray? Don't most of us focus the bulk of our requests on our grandchildren's health and happiness? You know, "And Lord, please give my grandchild a good day and keep her safe." There's nothing necessarily wrong with asking God to make our grandchildren healthy and happy, but surely there is more to praying for our grandchildren than that. If we limit most of our prayers for our grandchildren to their health and happiness, we might be asking for too little. The Bible shows us that God's priorities for our prayers go beyond the physical and emotional safety of our grandchildren.

When we read our Bibles, what can we learn about our priorities in praying for our grandchildren? What if we started with that line from Psalm 78:7 that is so central to this book on gospel-centered grandparenting: "[S]o that they [the next generation] should set their hope in God"? Isn't that one of God's primary objectives for us in our grandparenting, that we would have such an impact on the coming generations that they would set their hope in God? Well then, let's make that one of our regular, passionate prayer requests. "Lord, please work in my grandchild's heart so that he would not put his hope in his own abilities or achievements or in the deceptive, empty promises of this fallen world, but let him set his hope in you!"

It is important also that we give priority to asking the Lord to give our grandchildren new hearts, devoting ourselves to praying for their salvation. Over 300 years ago, the English Puritan pastor Matthew Henry wrote, "When a child is born, there is a candle lighted that must burn to eternity, either in heaven or hell; the consideration whereof should awaken us to pray with all possible earnestness for the salvation of their souls, next to our own."[1] A sobering reminder, isn't it? Let's devote ourselves "to pray with all possible earnestness for the salvation of their souls," trusting entirely in the merit of Jesus's life, death, and resurrection.

In addition to praying for their salvation, what are some other biblical priorities that should guide our prayers for our grandchildren? Many of the psalms are written prayers— prayers of rejoicing, prayers of desperate need, and prayers of lament. As you read through the psalms, could you to turn what you are reading into a praise or prayer for your grandchildren? And what about the apostle Paul's reports of how he prayed for the people he cared for? Paul writes:

For this reason I bow my knees before the Father, from whom every family in heaven and on earth is named, that according to the riches of his glory he may grant you to be strengthened with power through his Spirit in your inner being, so that Christ may dwell in your hearts through faith—that you, being rooted and grounded in love, may have strength to comprehend with all the saints what is the breadth and length and height and depth, and to know the love of Christ that surpasses knowledge, that you may be filled with all the fullness of God. (Ephesians 3:14–19)

And, that's just one of his recorded prayers! Also worthy of thoughtful consideration are the prayers found in Philippians 1:9–11, Colossians 1:9–14, Ephesians 1:15–23, and 2 Thessalonians 1:3. May they guide you in your prayers for your grandchildren.

Here are some ways to pray for our grandchildren that my wife and I adapted from work by Christian Grandparenting Network's National Prayer Co-director Lillian Penner,[2] as well as from Ginger Hubbard's book *Don't Make Me Count to Three.* Each prayer request has supporting scriptural references:

- Pray that they would honor and obey their parents, as well as those in authority over them (Ephesians 6:1–3; Hebrews 13:17).
- Pray that they would have a life-long love for God's Word (Psalms 1:2; 119:97, 165).
- Pray that the Lord would surround them with godly friends and role models (1 Corinthians 15:33; Proverbs 13:20; Proverbs 27:17).
- Pray that they would learn to humbly accept advice and gain understanding (Proverbs 15:31–32).

- Pray that the Lord would plant in their hearts a hunger and thirst for him (Psalm 42:1–2).
- Pray that the Lord would give them the Spirit of wisdom and revelation, so that they might know him better (Ephesians 1:17).
- Pray that the eyes of their hearts would be enlightened, in order that they might know the hope to which he has called them (Ephesians 1:18).
- Pray that they would always follow the truth and reject the lies of Satan (Proverbs 22:3; Titus 2:11–12).
- Pray that they would bear much fruit for God's glory (Galatians 5:22–23; Ephesians 2:10; 1 John 3:16–18).
- Pray that they would flee temptation (1 Corinthians 10:13; 2 Timothy 2:22–26).
- Pray that they would lean on God's grace in saying "no" to ungodliness and "yes" to godly living (Titus 2:11–13).
- Pray that they would be quick to listen, slow to speak, and slow to become angry (James 1:19).
- Pray that they would use their gifts and talents to honor the Lord (Proverbs 16:3; 1 Corinthians 10:31).
- Pray that they would have freedom from fear as they trust in the Lord (Psalm 56:13; 2 Thessalonians 3:16; 2 Timothy 1:7; 1 Peter 5:7).
- Pray that they would learn to be content with what they have (Philippians 4:12).
- Pray that they would acknowledge God and depend on his direction in life (Proverbs 3:5–6).
- Pray that the Lord would help them reflect the attitude of Christ in considering others better than themselves (Philippians 2:1–5).

- Pray that they would learn to do their best for the glory of God (Colossians 3:23).
- Pray that they would keep themselves sexually pure for their future spouses (1 Corinthians 10:8; Hebrews 13:4).
- Pray that the Lord would bring godly spouses into their lives (2 Corinthians 6:14–16).
- Pray that they would take captive every thought and make it obedient to Christ (2 Corinthians 10:5; Philippians 4:8).
- Pray that they would become more like Christ (Romans 8:28–29).

In addition to weaving biblical priorities into our prayers for our grandchildren, there will also be those personal, particular concerns that come along in life. One way to be intentional about loving our grandkids is to make a habit of asking our adult children how we can be praying for their children. As issues arise in our grandkids' lives, keeping open lines of communication can encourage their parents while helping us keep alive our active ministry of prayer.

We can also ask our grandchildren directly how we can be praying for them. Maybe they are struggling with getting along with a classmate or sibling or feeling anxiety about school. When we hear those concerns, we can assure them that we are listening to them and can make a point of praying and keeping in touch regarding what is going on with them.

In order to pray more consistently, it may help to keep some form of prayer journal. Some grandparents have found it helpful to have a page dedicated to each grandchild in their prayer journals, noting prayer requests and answers to those prayers. Wouldn't this provide a wonderful reminder not only to pray for our grandchildren, but to interact with them over the matters of their heart?

Praying with Our Grandchildren

What a privilege it is to get to pray *with* our grandchildren. When we do, we get to hear their hearts as they pray, and they get to hear ours. And, as a bonus, we have the opportunity to teach our grandchildren about prayer, gently guiding them in their own prayers and modeling how to pray.

Let's not miss those opportunities to pray with our grandchildren when they come for a visit. Even those grandchildren who are just learning to talk can be guided word by word to show gratitude for God's kindness in saying, "Thank-you-God-for-our-food. Amen!" If a grandchild has not been in the habit of praying or just seems hesitant, without being forceful, we grandparents can begin our prayer time by asking, "What can we thank God for?" The prayer requests will surely start as simple requests with the young grandchildren: "Thank you for our food. Thank you for Mommy. Thank you for Daddy." Let's encourage our grandchildren with words of affirmation after they pray. As the grandchildren grow, their prayers will become more thoughtful and, Lord willing, heartfelt. At our family gatherings, I often ask for a volunteer or two to pray before our meals. It's fine if more than one grandchild offers to pray. There's no requirement to have only one person pray, is there? We celebrate the blessing of having multiple family members praying at our table, sometimes with a representative from each generation.

When the grandkids come for an overnight stay, bedtimes provide wonderful opportunities for us to be intentional in pointing the young ones to the Lord through reading a Bible story, having a brief conversation about what we just read, and turning to the Lord in prayer. At those times, we like to reflect back on our day, discussing before we pray what we want to thank God for. And we talk briefly about tomorrow, discussing how we might ask for God's help for the coming day. As a grandpa, I like to use these times to involve each grandchild in the bedtime prayers. Rather than asking, "Who wants to pray?" which gives grandchildren the easy option of bowing out of the prayer time, I usually ask, "Tonight, should we pray youngest to oldest, or oldest to youngest?" Though not forced, ideally, everyone will pray—each grandchild plus Grandpa and Grandma. We can thank each of the grandchildren for praying, assure them of how much they are loved, give bedtime kisses, tuck them in, say "goodnight," and go get some much-needed rest ourselves!

There will be other opportunities to pray with our grandchildren. We can pray with them before an important event in their lives, such as a performance or athletic event they're involved in at school or church. We can pray with them when they show concern over a big test or when they're struggling to get along with a family member or friend. Those times when we're tending to "owies" that come with active children are great times to pause and pray for God to heal the injury.

As grandparents, we want to model in very tangible ways that we live in the presence of a sovereign, loving God who wants us to talk to him. Over time, this becomes a natural part of our relationship with our grandchildren. Don't be surprised if a grandchild comes and asks, "Grandpa or Grandma, can we pray about such and such?" Recently, while traveling together in the car, one of our grandsons asked, "Papa, will you pray for my teacher? Her father is dying, and, even though he will go to heaven, my teacher is sad." I gladly responded as I was driving, "Sure, Buddy. Let's pray right now," to which he replied, "Okay, but Papa, please don't close your eyes while you pray!"

But what if your grandchildren live far away, and you rarely have the opportunity to be physically present with them to pray? Well, let's not be hesitant to use technology as a gift from God, providing us with opportunities to pray with our grandchildren at a distance. Can you image the impact that this sort of intentional prayer can have on our grandchildren for life and for eternity? Yes, "The prayer of a righteous person [including, especially, grandparents] has great power as it is working" (James 5:16).

Discussion Questions and Action Steps for Chapter 5

Discussion Questions:

1. As you think about your own desires to grow as a gospel-centered grandparent, how would you like to pray for yourself? How would you like your spouse, kids, or fellow-grandparents to pray for you and your ministry of grandparenting?
2. What are some ways you want to pray for your grandchildren's parents?
3. As you think about your typical prayers for your grandchildren (Their safety? Happiness?), how might you want your prayers to grow after reading this chapter?
4. If you are in a grandparenting group, what prayer requests for your family would you like to share with your fellow grandparents?

Action Steps:

1. Start a prayer journal—either on paper or electronically—with an entry for each grandchild. You might want to have a place for both prayer requests and answers to prayer.
2. Ask your grandchildren's parents for prayer requests for themselves, as well as for their children.
3. Make a habit of regularly asking each of your grandchildren how you can be praying for them. If appropriate, seize the moment and pray for them there and then, either in person or over the phone.

4. If you have grandchildren old enough to have their own phones, how about sharing prayer requests and answers to prayer via text messages?

Chapter 6

Gospel Grandparenting in Today's Culture

The Challenge of Distance

In many cultures of the world, families live inter-generationally, with grandparents living near or even with their children, grand-children, and possibly great-grandchildren; but this is rarely the case in North America. America is such a mobile society. Many grandparents find themselves living at a great distance from their grandchildren. In fact, nearly half of American grandparents live at least 200 miles from one or more of their grandchildren.[3] Sometimes, it is the grandparent who has moved—maybe to a retirement community in order to enjoy a warmer climate. But usually it's the kids who have moved away to take on a new job in another community or maybe to move closer to the spouse's family.

So, how can you stay close to your grandchildren who live far from you? How can you have a meaningful relationship with grandchildren that you don't get to be with on a frequent basis? Maintaining—and even growing—a close relationship with family members who have moved away will cost the grandparent. It will cost time, effort, and money. There may be an emotional cost, too. You might be wrestling with a measure of emotional hurt, not wanting them to have moved away in the first place.

It can hurt to see our kids and grandkids move far away. How might the gospel provide a measure of hope and healing to a hurting grandparent's heart? May I ask you to spend some time reflecting on the wonder of your salvation? Think about it: Jesus Christ left his home in heaven to come here to redeem us. Might we reflect him in taking the initiative to lovingly, sacrificially pursue a relationship with family members who are far away? The gospel enables and empowers us to love sacrificially. Ultimately, our family belongs to him, not to us. He may well have purposes for their move that we are not yet aware of. Let's honor him with hearts of humble submission.

Gospel-empowered, Christ-reflecting grandparents can take the initiative to nurture a close relationship with our long-distance kids and grandkids, even when that requires a sacrifice of time, effort, and finances. Here are some ideas on how to intentionally pursue a close relationship with your long-distance grandchildren:

- *Planned visits to their home*: Are there particular times each year that you can set as a "repeat annually" on your calendar for a visit? Depending on distance and available funds (and the number of your grandchildren!), might you be able to make it a family tradition to visit your long-distance grandchildren on their birthdays? Are there other annual events in your family that would make a good time for a visit, such as an end-of-the-school-year celebration or Grandparents' Day at the grandkids' school? Even if this requires some serious funding for travel, it might be workable by planning ahead and making a line-item in your annual budget for visits to the grandchildren. You may find that the expense of time and money will be worth the effort, even if it means giving up some optional items or activities that you were planning to spend on yourself.

- *Planned visits to your home*: Might you be able to plan an annual family gathering or two in your home—maybe Thanksgiving or Christmas, for example? As the older generation, it might be really meaningful if you were able and willing to invest the time and resources necessary to make this happen. Maybe you could offer to assist your kids financially, if necessary, to make their visit happen. If the space available for overnight guests in your home is a bit tight, instead of treating the crowded conditions as a burden, why not treat it as a fun adventure? Build excitement in anticipation of their visit by talking to the grandkids about "camping" in Grandma and Grandpa's living room. Demonstrate how much you've been looking forward to being together by having family photos around the house from a previous visit. Have some of your grandchildren's favorite books and toys ready for them to enjoy during their visit. And how about some fun inter-generational activities?

- *Family vacation trips*: Why not budget time and money for a vacation trip with your kids and grandkids? You might be able to splurge on a big trip that includes multiple days at an amusement park like Disney World. But if the costs involved for plane tickets, hotels, meals, and passes to the park are beyond your financial means, don't discount the possibility of less-expensive options. Is there a state or national park that you and your family could meet at, exploring the park's high-lights together, making memories camping, hiking the trails, cooking on a camp stove, and telling stories around the campfire? Or perhaps a friend has a cabin or cottage you could rent or borrow for a few days as a fun gathering place for you and your family? Brainstorm the options. Involve your kids and grandkids in thinking of some possibilities. You will be investing in making enduring memories with your children and grandchildren.

- *Use available technology for video chats*: What a blessing it is to live in this era, when we have the possibility to connect with our long-distance family members through live video calls *for free*! We grandparents can remember the day when such a thought would have been considered science fiction, but now, with an internet connection on both ends, we can call family members 100 miles away or 1,000 miles away or even 10,000 miles away and have immediate voice and visual conversations. If distance is keeping you from being with your grandchildren physically, you can be intentional in using this means of being in virtual proximity. Talk to your kids, getting their input on the best times to make video calls to your grandchildren. Maybe you would want to schedule a regular time each week—or even more frequently—to connect with your grand-children this way. If your grandchildren are younger, especially keep in mind the importance of discussing with your grandkids' parents when might be the best time to call. They know their nap and meal times. And, of course, remember the different time zones you have to work around.

Be intentional with your calls. What questions do you want to ask your grandkids? Is there a special project they've been working on that you could ask to see? What stories do you want to tell them? Would you like to read them a story during your video chat? Work on a Bible memory verse together? Pray for them? And don't forget those video calls for special events such as birthdays, the first day of school, holidays, etc. If your grandchild is in an event at school or church, maybe one of the parents could connect to you virtually during that event. There are so many possibilities to strengthen your ties to your long-distance grandchildren through technology.

- *Send mail and packages*: Remember letters? I mean, real, handwritten letters that come in the mail. Children love getting mail with their own name on the envelope. Think through the various times during the year that you could send a card or letter to your grandchild— for a birthday, Valentine's Day, Easter, Christmas, the first day of school, or just to congratulate him or her for a special accomplishment. When you write, make it thoughtfully personal, maybe pointing out how you see God's grace in your grandchild's life or writing out a blessing. And, packages—what child doesn't love getting a package in the mail from Grandpa and Grandma? Maybe you're sending a birthday gift or Christmas package. If so, how about asking your kids to let you know when the package has arrived and is about to be opened? Maybe you can connect via a video call to be there virtually when your grandchild opens up your package. Wouldn't that be fun?

- *With your kids' permission, consider ways to connect with your long-distance grandchildren spiritually:* Even if you are separated from your grandkids by hundreds of miles, you can still engage with them spiritually. For example, if your grandchild is old enough to read, why not work out a plan in which you and your grandchild are on the same daily Bible reading plan? You might even consider giving a gift of a devotional Bible that has a reading plan and simultaneously getting an identical copy for yourself. Then, you can discuss with your grandchild what your plan will be, like reading the same daily passages, then interacting through email, text, or video call over what you've been learning together from God's Word. Maybe you could have a regular time each month or week in which you ask your grandchild for specific prayer requests. Then, having prayed for those concerns, check later with your grandchild on how the Lord is answering them. It takes intentionality, but these shared spiritual endeavors can have a deep bonding effect on the grandparent-grandchild relationship, even if many miles separate you.
- *Move closer:* I know, this sounds extreme. But is moving closer to your grandchildren a possibility? For some grandparents it is. Maybe you've retired from your job, are no longer caring for your own elderly parent, or are otherwise not tied to your current community any longer. Rather than picking up and moving to a sunny retirement community where you spend your days pursuing your pleasures, why not consider moving closer to your grandchildren? Remember that our Lord left his home in heaven to come dwell among us (John

1:14). He didn't move to our fallen planet for his own sake. He did it for us. Of course, you and your spouse will want to prayerfully consider this major decision before you make specific plans, and you will want to have an open conversation with your kids as to whether they would welcome such a move. If God seems to be directing you toward moving to a home closer to your grandchildren, ask him to help you make the transition well so that you can impact your children's and grandchildren's lives in eternally significant ways.

The Challenge of Divorce

I can still remember a dear friend of mine pouring out his heart about the pain of his own divorce. He called it "a living death." Through the tears, he explained that when you lose a loved one in physical death, there's deep pain, but there's also a sense of finality. But in divorce, there's the death of a relationship, but there's no finality. The pain goes on and on. It can feel like a "living death."

Maybe you can relate to my friend's anguish. Maybe your family has been torn apart through divorce, and it feels to you like a death. Maybe it was your own divorce from your ex-spouse that continues to make relationships with your kids and grandkids more complicated than you would have ever desired. Or maybe one of your kids has gone through a divorce, making your relationship with your own grandchildren painfully challenging. So, what's a grandparent to do when the family has been torn apart by divorce? Are there any applications of the gospel that can help?

What if one of your own kids and his or her spouse has gone through divorce—maybe an ugly, painful divorce—leaving casualties on the battlefield of your family relationships?

What can you do as a grandparent in that difficult situation? What does God call you to, and how might the gospel enable you as a parent and grandparent to reflect him, his character, and his grace in the confusion and anguish of an extended family torn apart by divorce?

First, let me encourage you to open your own hurting heart to your heavenly Father. What truth does 1 Peter 5:6–7 remind us of? "Humble yourselves, therefore, under the mighty hand of God so that at the proper time he may exalt you, casting all your anxieties on him, because he cares for you." If your heart is aching right now with the pain and complications that have been inflicted on your family due to the divorce of one of your kids, may I ask you to pause in your reading and reflect on that astonishing phrase at the end of 1 Peter 5:7? "He cares for you." Think about that. The sovereign King of the universe is also your heavenly Father. He has already demonstrated his mind-blowing, heart-melting, eternity-changing love for you in sending his precious Son to die in your place (Romans 5:8). Now, view your current family relationships looking through the lens of that gospel truth. Though your family is going through painful times, you are not outside of your heavenly Father's love. His love for you has already been demonstrated in the manger of Bethlehem and the cross of Calvary. He cares for you as his beloved child. With your heart anchored in that love, "cast all your anxieties on him." Go into your heavenly Father's throne room and lay your pain and confusion on his divine lap, knowing that he is both willing and able to care for your situation.

Second, let me also encourage you, as you are in this painful situation, to stay close to Christian friends who can pray for you and point you to Jesus as you weather this storm that feels like it's going to sink your family. Isolating ourselves in our pain is not a good idea. We need our spiritual family, the body of Christ, when we are going through especially difficult times.

Third, apply gospel truths in guarding your heart against bitterness toward your child and/or child-in-law for the pain they have brought upon you and the family, especially the life-jolting pain the grandchildren must now be experiencing. Often in these situations, in our pain, we want to blame someone. Any attempts to make the one we see as "the guilty party" pay for his or her "crimes" against the family will probably drive the family further apart—and this could have serious unforeseen consequences for your grandchildren. We must remind ourselves of the gospel truth that none of us earned God's love. He loved us while we were still sinners (Romans 5:8). Our love for our kids or kids-in-law is not something they must earn. First John 4:11 prompts us, "If God so loved us, we also ought to love one another." Verses 19–21 then grab our attention, "We love because he first loved us. If anyone says, 'I love God,' and hates his brother, he is a liar; for he who does not love his brother whom he has seen cannot love God whom he has not seen. And this commandment we have from him: whoever loves God must also love his brother [or ex-son-in-law or ex-daughter-in-law]." Ask the Lord to help you love as he has loved you.

Fourth, remember that your grandchildren may need you now more than ever. As the older generation, we grandparents can be anchors during times of family tumult. The grandchildren are feeling the fear of losing their family as they have known it. They might be wrestling with anger, blaming their parents for not working out their problems, or blaming themselves for the family breakup. Listen to their hearts carefully and compassionately. Speak gently, acknowledging the pain and reminding them of God's love and yours. In some situations, you may need to say "no" to some things in your life for a season so that you can give extra attention to your hurting family.

Grandfathers, what if your son or ex-son-in-law is now largely missing from the picture due to a divorce or marital separation? This may be a situation that requires you to step up your involvement in the lives of your grandkids. They may have increased need for a manly example and involvement in their daily lives, filling in the gap left by the grandchildren's absent father. It might be appropriate to speak to your daughter or daughter-in-law, asking her input on how she would appreciate your increased involvement in the lives of her children. Grandmothers, you may be especially needed in the lives of your grandchildren who have "lost" a mother through divorce or separation. A grandmother's presence, involvement, and patient endurance despite the new, uncomfortable situation of family disharmony can be a profound assurance of God's continued care, even if we cannot reverse or fully nullify the painful effects of divorce. If your own family has not experienced the situation of an absentee father or mother, is there a family in your community or church that could benefit from the involvement of a surrogate grandparent?

When there has been a painful divorce, we must not take sides when speaking to our grandkids. This is difficult because we will inevitably have feelings and judgments regarding the situation. But we must take care to not pronounce on the situation or demean those involved, especially in the presence of your grandchildren. Doing so will only cause additional harm, for you're talking about one of their parents, and children should not be placed in the disorienting position of having to form judgments against those to whom they look for guidance and security. Instead, leaning on God's grace, we grandparents must obey the commands of Ephesians 4:29–32, "Let no corrupting talk come out of your mouths, but only such as is good for building up, as fits the occasion, that it may give grace to those who hear. . . . Let all bitterness and wrath and anger and clamor and slander be put away from you, along with all malice. Be kind to one another, tenderhearted, forgiving one another, as God in Christ forgave you."

In some situations, your ex-child-in-law may have custody of your grandchildren and attempt to inhibit your contact with your own grandkids. You may choose to politely request legal visitation rights as a grandparent, but be careful to not inflame the situation or defame the name of Christ by "fighting fire with fire." If you do that, everyone gets burned. Instead, in such situations, we are called to patiently love and pray, staying as involved as we are able and seeking, as much as possible, to let our grandchildren know of our continued love.

But what if it was your own divorce that has added layers of complexity to your relationship with your grandchildren? Maybe you have been divorced from the grandkids' grandmother since your own kids were young. Or your divorce might have taken place in more recent years, after already becoming a grandparent. Either way, when Grandma and Grandpa don't live together because of divorce, there are special challenges relationally and functionally that have to be worked through in order to have a God-honoring relationship with your grandchildren.

So, how does the gospel help you work through the painful effects of your own divorce in regard to grandparenting? If you are indeed a child of God through Jesus Christ, remind yourself of his kindness to you in giving you his Holy Spirit. As you face the heart issues and functional challenges of living with the consequences of your divorce, you may feel, "I can't do this alone!" And you're right. You can't do it alone. But, you're not alone. God, in his amazing grace, is with you (Psalm 23:4). And he has given you his family, the church, in whose holy company God offers strength and comfort in the midst of our many difficulties (1 Peter 4:8–10). And what does God's

Word remind us of in Galatians 5:22–26? "But the fruit of the Spirit is love, joy, peace, patience, kindness, goodness, faithfulness, gentleness, self-control; against such things there is no law. And those who belong to Christ Jesus have crucified the flesh with its passions and desires. If we live by the Spirit, let us also keep in step with the Spirit. Let us not become conceited, provoking one another, envying one another."

"Keep in step with the Spirit." This presupposes that, in our difficulties, God the Spirit is walking with us, and he wants to help us keep pace with him, not turning aside to bitterness and sin but pressing on toward conformity to the image of Jesus Christ (2 Corinthians 3:18). As God, through our difficulty, is in the processes of faithfully transforming us to reflect the character of our Savior, the Spirit is working in us to bear, eventually, the fruit of "love, joy, peace, patience, kindness, goodness, faithfulness, gentleness, self-control." As we read God's Word and seek to grow more like Christ, let us remember that God is gracious, powerful, and ultimately victorious. He hears our prayers, and he will answer.

The Challenge of Accepting Grandchildren Through Remarriage or Adoption

What if there has been remarriage? Maybe you have remarried after a divorce or after the death of a spouse, and your new spouse already had grandchildren. Or maybe your child has married someone who already had children. What should your relationship be with these "inherited" grandchildren?

It's quite likely that you have not had the privilege of building a relationship with these grandchildren before the new marriage. How do you build a relationship with someone who wasn't born as your grandchild, especially a new grandchild who may be a bit older? And what should your role be in light of the fact that these grandchildren may already have established relationships with their natural grandparents?

What are some gospel truths that might enrich our relationships with special grandchildren? Well, for a start, let's recall the truth that we were adopted by our heavenly Father. He chose us to be part of his family. Ephesians 1:4–5 reminds us, "[H]e chose us in him before the foundation of the world, that we should be holy and blameless before him. In love he predestined us for adoption as sons through Jesus Christ." God welcomed us into his family because of Jesus Christ and what he did on our behalf. In light of God's welcome, surely we ought to be similarly disposed to those who might enter into our families through various, even surprising avenues. Romans 15:7 says, "[W]elcome one another as Christ has welcomed you, for the glory of God." There is no reason to assume a standoffish posture toward newly gained grandchildren. God has not been standoffish with us, has he? He chose to move toward us, even when we were not moving toward him.

By God's grace, we can reflect him as we choose to move toward these new grandchildren. We can say "welcome to the family" with sincere love and joy, and we can do so face to face or in a letter or special card. Why not mark on your calendar special dates for that new grandchild, such as birthdays and special events, so that you can surprise her with timely expressions of thoughtful love? And don't forget to include your new grandchildren in your regular prayers for your family.

You may need to demonstrate special compassion and patience with the child (or teen) who is warming up to you slowly or even deliberately keeping their distance. Be neither forceful, nor passive. Gently demonstrate love and acceptance through words and intentional acts of kindness. Let the child determine the pace of growth in your relationship. Don't be offended if the child doesn't immediately accept your love. Blending a family takes time—lots of time. Take the high road. After all, you are the older one involved in this relationship.

Beware of the pain that can be caused by showing favoritism to "natural" grandchildren while treating "new" grandchildren as second class. To be candid, the way these children came into your family may be less than ideal. Your adult child may have made poor decisions when ending a previous marriage or when marrying his or her spouse. Whatever the situation, it is not the children's fault. Our calling in this situation is, like God, to stretch a wing of protection over these children, offering them as much loving support as they are willing to receive (Psalm 57:1; Ruth 2:12).

Gladly celebrate the new grandchild's relationship with his or her other sets of grandparents. Love knows no competition. Speak well of the other adults in the family, including the other grandparents and any ex-daughter-in-law or son-in-law. Empowered by God's grace, seek to live out the directive of Colossians 4:6, "Let your speech always be gracious." Struggling with living out that command? Maybe it's time to pray that ancient prayer of Psalm 141:3, "Set a guard, O LORD, over my mouth; keep watch over the door of my lips!" He will help you. And show Christlike patience in sharing time with the other sets of grandparents. It's quite likely that the birth grandparents have established traditions of when their extended family gathers for holidays and vacations. In those situations, don't start a tug-of-war with the other grandparents, but look for ways to begin your own traditions with your new grandchildren, deferring to one another in reverence of Christ (Ephesians 5:21).

Has there been an adoption in your family? While adopted grandchildren are usually quickly accepted and even celebrated by grandparents, it's possible that you find your heart just a bit more reserved than it is with natural grandchildren. Such feelings are common, but they cannot be allowed to go unaddressed. Have you taken your feelings to God in prayer, asking him to help you be like him in loving without partiality

(James 2:9; Ephesians 6:9)? Are you struggling to accept fully a newly adopted grandchild who doesn't carry your family genes or who may have a different racial or ethnic identity than you? The New Testament is clear that the kingdom of God is a multiethnic family, in which all share as equals (Galatians 3:28; Revelation 7:9–10). Since our earthly families are given to us as mirrors of this heavenly reality (Ephesians 3:15), let us pray for our hearts to reflect more fully the love of the God who, despite the vast difference between him and us, adopts us as his own through Jesus Christ (Isaiah 57:15; Romans 8:15).

The Challenge of Taking in the Grandchildren

Maybe your grandparenting has taken a radical turn and you have become the primary caregiver for your grandchild. You are not alone in facing the many challenges of "starting over" with raising another generation of children—something you may have never envisioned having to do when your own children were born a generation ago. Currently in America, about 2.7 million grandparents are the primary caregivers for their grandchildren. And the numbers of grandparents raising their grandchildren is growing.[4]

Sometimes grandparents may need to take the responsibility for the daily care of their grandchildren. This may be due to any number of reasons, including the death of the children's parents, military deployment, or other instances in which the parents are unable or unwilling to care for their children. So, what is a Christian grandparent to do when she finds herself being not only the grandparent, but the surrogate parent? Former dreams of having more time and money to spend on travel and hobbies may fade when we receive the unexpected call to return to parenting mode. Suddenly, the grandparent who is thrust back into parenting is faced with new challenges emotionally, economically, and logistically. For the sake of the grandchildren, we grandparents must move forward, even as we may be grieving the situation that led to this unexpected responsibility.

Are there government or community programs that could offer assistance? Spending some time searching the web for resources available to grandparents raising their grandchildren may prove helpful. Some grandparents in this situation have gone through the steps to become licensed as foster parents, opening doors to some assistance from the state. This could be a real help for grandparents in limited income situations. (According to current census figures, about one-fifth of grand-parents raising grandchildren have incomes that fall below the poverty line.)[5] Your local church may be able to help. Talk to your church leadership to find out how the body of Christ might be able to come alongside you as you carry an unexpected burden.

What practical relevance does the gospel of Jesus Christ have on this drastic life change that a growing number of grandparents are facing? Clearly, grandparents being thrust into raising their grandchildren is a situation that calls for great personal sacrifice. Time, money, and energy that the grandparent had hopes of spending in one direction are now redirected toward helping raise someone else's children. Most Christians are familiar with the classic expression of God's love for us as found in John 3:16, "For God so loved the world, that he gave his only Son." But how does his sacrificial love for us impact our lives, in turn? Are you familiar with another "3:16"? First John 3:16 explains, "By this we know love, that he laid down his life for us, and we ought to lay down our lives for the brothers." Might we paraphrase that last verse, "and we ought to lay down our lives for our *grandchildren*"? His love for us motivates and empowers us to show sacrificial love to others: "And so we know *and rely on* the love God has for us" (1 John 4:16 NIV, emphasis added). Our loving Lord can empower grandparents in this challenging life situation to reflect him as they help raise their grandchildren.

If you are faced with the unexpected responsibility of raising your grandchildren, let me encourage you to keep your eyes on the end of your journey, challenging though your road may be. Not only will you have had increased opportunities to pour into your grandchildren God's love and grace, but your royal heavenly Father has been watching you all along the way.

> "The King will say to those on his right, 'Come, you who are blessed by my Father, inherit the kingdom prepared for you from the foundation of the world. For I was hungry and you gave me food, I was thirsty and you gave me drink, I was a stranger and you welcomed me, I was naked and you clothed me, I was sick and you visited me, I was in prison and you came to me.' Then the righteous will answer him, saying, 'Lord, when did we see you hungry and feed you, or thirsty and give you drink? And when did we see you a stranger and welcome you, or naked and clothe you? And when did we see you sick or in prison and visit you?' And the King will answer them, 'Truly, I say to you, as you did it to one of the least of these my brothers [your own grandchildren?], you did it to me.'" (Matthew 25:34–40)

And then, those most-blessed words any human being could ever hear, "Well done, good and faithful servant. You have been faithful over a little; I will set you over much. Enter into the joy of your master" (Matthew 25:23).

The Challenge of Defiant Relationships

What is the grandparent to do when his or her own heart is aching from a severely broken relationship with her own child, child-in-law, ex-child-in-law, or even her own teen or adult grandchild? Maybe your older grandchild is acting like he doesn't even want you or your God in his life. Or maybe your child or child-in-law has built walls around his family—including your own grandchildren—with you on the outside, rarely and reluctantly unlocking the door to let you in for an awkward, all-too-brief visit. What kind of involvement can a grandparent have in a family broken by painful relationships? What light might the gospel provide in that depressing darkness?

Relying on the gospel of Jesus Christ enables us to do the necessary work of first exploring what our own contribution to the family brokenness and barriers might be. Our natural (and sinful) tendency is to exonerate ourselves while finding blame in others. If we miss the truth that our standing before God is based not on our own performance but the performance of Christ, we will live with a bent toward self-justification and seeking other people to blame for our problems. But the gospel reminds us to rely on the righteousness of Christ rather than our assumed self-righteousness as we explore possible paths to reconciliation with our estranged family members. And the gospel empowers us to obey the directive of our Lord when he said, "First take the log out of your own eye, and then you will see clearly to take the speck out of your brother's eye" (Matthew 7:5).

As you humble yourself before God, ask him to search your heart and to show you your sin. Confess those sins he brings to your attention, asking his forgiveness and help in overcoming them. Is the Holy Spirit directing you to seek forgiveness from your child or grandchild for your part in the family conflict? Ask the Lord to guide you as you carefully think through your approach. It might be advisable to write out what you are planning to say, reading and re-reading it a few times, maybe even getting the input of a wise Christian friend before proceeding. Is your confession of your sin free of self-justification (often cloaked as "explanations") for your sin or veiled critiques of others? True restoration comes—and sometimes comes very slowly—only through true humility.

But what if your child or grandchild still holds you at arm's length or even completely blocks you from family involvement after you have humbled yourself and sought forgiveness for your part in the broken or strained relationship? Don't strike back at your grandchild when he responds in this way, even if you are treated with disrespect or spoken to in mean-spirited ways. Remember whose you are, and entrust your broken heart and your broken family to the One who understands:

> For to this you have been called, because Christ also suffered for you, leaving you an example, so that you might follow in his steps. He committed no sin, neither was deceit found in his mouth. When he was reviled, he did not revile in return; when he suffered, he did not threaten, but continued entrusting himself to him who judges justly. (1 Peter 2:21–23)

In the meantime, continue to pray for God's gracious intervention in your family as you bear faithful witness to the patient love of God.

One friend of ours who was completely blocked out of her grandchildren's lives by the painful decision of the parent, nevertheless continued to show Christ-honoring love in a hopeful, creative way. Each birthday and holiday she wrote a special note to each of those grandchildren with whom she was not allowed to have any interaction. She bought them each a gift on those significant occasions, carefully wrapping it and placing it in a special box labeled with the grandchild's name. Her prayerful hope was that one day the Lord would open the door to her grandchildren, allowing her to have the relationship she longed for so dearly. Even if the parent barred the door to her grandchildren during all of their growing-up years, one day those grandchildren would be adults. On that day, her hope was to present each of those formerly-estranged grandchildren with his special box, showing him at last that she had been loving him all along.

Maybe I haven't touched on your specific challenges as a grandparent. Maybe you're struggling to know how to be a grandparent to a grandchild born out of wedlock or a grandchild with physical and/or mental disabilities. Or maybe you are wondering what your role should be if your kids have taken in foster children. Though this book may have its limits in covering every particular situation, remember that God's love and power are not limited. As you face the various challenges of grandparenting, begin by recalling the gospel: How does God treat you? What is the nature and shape of his love for you? How can you reflect his grace as you seek to be like him in your grandparenting? Though your situation might be difficult, it's not impossible. "And God is able to make all grace abound to you, so that having all sufficiency in all things at all times, you may abound in every good work" (2 Corinthians 9:8). That's a lot of "alls," isn't it?

Discussion Questions and Action Steps for Chapter 6

Discussion Questions:

1. What are some challenges you are facing as a grandparent? What makes them so hard?
2. What are some ways you have stayed connected to grandchildren who live some distance away? Are there ways you could improve your connectedness, now that you've read this chapter?
3. What would have to happen for you to be able to visit your long-distance grandchildren? What could you be doing to make that visit possible?

4. Has your family been impacted by divorce? What special challenges have you experienced because of divorce in your extended family?
5. What truths of the gospel have you found helpful in your difficulties as a grandparent?

Action Steps:

1. If you have not already done so, download whatever app is necessary for you to have video calls with your long-distance grandchildren. Begin scheduling regular video calls.
2. Do you need to pursue reconciliation with a family member? Discuss and pray about this with a Christian friend, then make that call, requesting an opportunity to have a humble, loving, heart-to-heart conversation.
3. Are you in a small group or accountability group at your church? If so, be open about the struggles you are facing in your family, requesting prayer support as a parent or grandparent. If you're not in a group, what do you need to do to join one?
4. Seek out the fellowship of other grandparents and pray for one another as you face difficulties and challenges, asking the Lord to remind you of the power and promises of the gospel.

Chapter 7

How Do I Leave a Godly Legacy?

HOW DOES THAT quip go? "What you *are* speaks so loudly I can't hear what you *say*." That retort, or at least something similar, is sometimes spoken by someone frustrated with perceived hypocrisy—especially hypocrisy seen in the life of someone in authority and trying to give counsel. Words of advice fall flat when given by a person seen as not living by his or her own standards. Words are powerful, but the effectiveness of those words rests on the life example of the person speaking them. Our words will be either enhanced or diminished by the example of our lives.

As grandparents, we want to leave a legacy for our grandchildren—not just a legacy of money or things, but a legacy of faith, love, and dependence on Jesus. Here's a heart-searching exercise: Imagine that you have passed away, and the pastor presiding at your funeral asks your now-adult grandchildren to give a testimony at the funeral of the impact you had on their lives. What will your grandchildren say at your funeral? What do you *hope* they will say?

Recently, a couple of my fellow pastors and I had the privilege of leading the funeral of a much-loved, godly lady in our church who died at the age of eighty. Her husband of sixty-one years, her children, and her grandchildren filled the first few rows. Several family members shared precious memories with smiles on their faces and tears on their cheeks. But as I listened, the words of one granddaughter in particular struck my own heart as a grandfather. This twenty-something granddaughter said, "Oh, how Grandma loved us. But, you know what? She loved Jesus even more!" My first thought as I sat listening to this heart-felt testimony was, "Wow! What a legacy to leave for your family! What a godly impact Grandma had on her granddaughter." There had been something in the way this dear lady lived daily life and the way she related to her family that made that impression on her grandchildren. As I sat there in that funeral service, I began to ask myself, "I wonder what my own grandchildren will say at *my* funeral? Would they be able to say something like that about me—that the primary legacy I left them was my love for Jesus?" Humbling. I began to ask myself, "What would have to be true of my life for that to happen?"

There is great power in a godly example, isn't there? That was the point of this proverb from the lips of Jesus: "A disciple is not above his teacher, but everyone when he is fully trained will be like his teacher" (Luke 6:40). Jesus was not painting a verbal picture of a classroom setting with rows of desks and a teacher standing up front lecturing. He was alluding to the example that he himself was setting by his way of life with his disciples. When Jesus said to those Galilean fishermen, "Come follow me," he was inviting them to follow him as their spiritual mentor, inviting them to learn about the kingdom of God as they lived life together.

As grandparents, let's meditate on Jesus's maxim for a moment: "Everyone when he is fully trained will be like his teacher." How does that apply to our role as grandparents? Well, over the course of time, as our grandchildren spend time with us, we rub off on them. To some degree, our lives begin to be replicated in the lives of our grandchildren. In some ways, our grandchildren become like us. They will reflect our character, our priorities, and our perspectives on life and eternity. It's not just what we *say* to our grandkids that can leave an impact. It's not just the activities we *do* with them. It's who we *are*. Sobering, isn't it?

As grandparents, we need to give serious thought to the legacy that we are leaving for the coming generations. In several places, the writers of the Bible were led by the Holy Spirit to draw the readers' attention to the power of a legacy of life, especially in how the lives on one generation helped shape the lives of the coming generations. The author of the book of Hebrews urges his readers, "Remember your leaders, those who spoke to you the word of God. Consider the outcome of their way of life, and imitate their faith" (Hebrews 13:7). He's stirring up the memories of believers, not only to recall the verbal lessons taught by their leaders but to give intentional, thoughtful recollection of their life-legacies that will encourage similar lives of faith. He knew the power of godly examples on the lives of the coming generations.

The apostle Paul likewise drew attention specifically to the power of a grandmother's godly example when he wrote to his closest protégé, Timothy. At the beginning of 2 Timothy, Paul reflected, "I am reminded of your sincere faith, a faith that dwelt first in your grandmother Lois and your mother Eunice and now, I am sure, dwells in you as well" (2 Timothy 1:5). The apostle was clearly honoring the impact that Timothy's godly grandmother and mother had on his life, acknowledging God's grace at work in the transmission of a life of faith from one generation to the next. Isn't that the implication of Paul's exhortation to Timothy a bit later in the letter? "But as for you, continue in what you have learned and have firmly believed, knowing from whom you learned it and how from childhood you have been acquainted with the sacred writings, which are able to make you wise for salvation through faith in Christ Jesus" (2 Timothy 3:14–15). Paul was not only reminding Timothy of the words of life he had learned as a boy growing up; he was also drawing Timothy's recollection back to the people from whom he had learned the gospel—his own godly grandmother and mother (and also Paul himself). There was power added to Paul's counsel, urging Timothy to remember the spiritual legacy he had been blessed with in his family context. God had used the gospel-teaching of a godly grandmother, given increased impact by her gospel-reflecting example, in shaping the life of young Timothy—a man used greatly by God in the spread of the gospel. Now, that's a legacy worth investing in as grandparents, the legacy of a godly example.

As we grandparents pursue Christ with gospel motivated passion, what fruit of the gospel should we be praying for in our own lives—fruit that will serve as a Christ-reflecting legacy for our grandchildren? Spending some time in Titus 2 may be helpful. In this chapter, Paul describes what the everyday life of Christians in various life situations should look like.

Let's start with grandfathers. What character traits should be evident in the lives of older men? Paul directs in Titus 2:2, "Older men are to be . . ."

- *Sober-minded:* That means that we older guys should be clear thinking, having a balanced perspective on what's happening around us. By God's grace, we grandfathers should resist reactionary attitudes in life or ranting and raving about frustrations we are feeling in our family situations, in our jobs, or, especially, in the world of economics and politics. Instead, trusting in our sovereign God, we can process life's happenings in a calm, sober-minded way and show the younger generations what it means to deal with the ups and

downs of life with wisdom and a calm trust in
God's unseen presence with us.

- *Self-controlled:* Our grandchildren should be able
  to see in us grandfathers a gospel-empowered
  control over our appetites, our use of time and
  money, our words, and our tempers. If we are out
  of control in one or more areas of our lives, we will
  show the young ones that the gospel has no real,
  practical effectiveness in our daily life. That is, we
  will show ourselves to be hypocrites.
- *Sound in faith:* We grandfathers should have a
  growing, healthy grip on the truths of God's Word,
  having learned through the years that the Bible is
  trustworthy. As we hold on to Christ ourselves,
  we can be anchors to our grandchildren when it
  comes to believing God's Word and can model for
  the coming generations the truth that God is who
  he says he is, and he does what he says he will do.
- *Sound in love:* The descriptive phrase common in
  our culture, "grumpy old men," should not come
  to mind when grandchildren reflect on the lives of
  their Christian grandfathers. When God's grace
  gets a grip on the life of an older man, he tends to
  be gracious, not grouchy. One practical overflow
  of the gospel's effect on the lives of older men is
  that they have a healthy love for other people. They
  are "sound in love."
- *Sound in steadfastness:* The pains, griefs, and disappointments that come from living for decades
  in this fallen world can make some grandfathers
  downright negative and pessimistic. But older men
  who know the God of grace have lives marked by
  a healthy endurance. The God-centered hope that

fills their hearts is evident in their steady conversations and lifestyles.

And what about grandmothers? Enabled by God's grace,
what kind of legacy can Christian grandmothers leave for the
coming generations? Let's look at Titus 2:3–4. "Older women
likewise are to be . . ."

- *Reverent in behavior:* The picture presented in this
  character trait is that of a woman who views her
  whole life as being an act of worship to God. Here
  is an older woman who is very conscious of God's
  mercies to her and lives daily life with gratitude,
  presenting to God the hours of her day as an act of
  worship (Romans 12:1–2).
- *Not slanderers:* The godly grandmother does not
  deliberately say things that might hurt the repu-
  tation of another person, even if that person has
  brought grief to the family. She guards her mouth,
  speaking only words that are "good for building
  up, as fits the occasion, that it may give grace to
  those who hear" (Ephesians 4:29).
- *She teaches what is good:* A Christ-honoring
  grandmother spends time learning from God's
  Word, then processes what she is learning, looking
  for life-applications she can pass on to the coming
  generations. Teaching from God's Word is a priority in her interactions with her grandchildren.
- *She gives special attention to training the younger
  women in her life:* What an awesome privilege
  grandmothers have! Godly grandmothers are
  called by God to be involved in discipling their
  daughters and granddaughters (and other younger
  women), training them in how to apply the gospel

to daily life, relationships, and responsibilities
(Titus 2:4–5). Of course, as the example of Timothy shows, this work isn't limited to training young
women (2 Timothy 1:5)! Godly grandmothers
impact their sons and grandsons, too.

So, what empowers this growth of character in the lives
of grandparents? Is it a matter of mere determination? "Just
do it?" Let's keep reading a bit longer in Titus 2. There's a
connecting word in verse 11 that adds hope and help in this
pursuit of leaving a godly legacy. Do you see it? It's the word
"for." After painting pictures of what the everyday lives of
ordinary Christians in various life situations should look like,
the apostle Paul adds these encouraging words about God's
extraordinary gospel: "*For* the grace of God has appeared,
bringing salvation for all people, training us to renounce
ungodliness and worldly passions, and to live self-controlled,
upright, and godly lives in the present age" (Titus 2:11–12).
Ordinary Christians can live extraordinary lives because they
are empowered by God's extraordinary grace. Not only *should*
we grow in godly character, but we *can. We can change. We
can grow*—no matter how old we are! God has given us his
grace—grace that "trains us" to live "self-controlled, upright,
and godly lives in the present age." We are not stuck, fellow
grandparents. As Christians, there's no reason to have a defeat-
ist attitude, "Well, that's just the way I am. You can't teach an
old dog new tricks." Listen: We're not dogs. We are redeemed
image-bearers of the God who has given us his amazing grace,
not only for initial salvation, but for the ongoing transformation of our daily lives.

So, how does God do that? By what means does he continue to grow us in grace so that we can live "godly lives in
the present age" (Titus 2:12)—lives that leave a godly legacy
to the coming generations? Clearly, the Word of God is a

primary tool in the hand of our gracious God as he shapes our lives. Second Timothy 3:16–17 reminds us, "All Scripture is breathed out by God and profitable for teaching, for reproof, for correction, and for training in righteousness, that the man of God may be complete, equipped for every good work." The Bible is "profitable"—useful—in shaping our lives. So, as Christians who want to continue to grow in grace, even in this latter season of our lives, we make a point to block out time to personally read our Bibles. And with our minds engaged and our hearts hungry, we determine to learn as much as we can when the Bible is taught and preached in our local churches. We are thankful to have the benefit of accessing books and podcasts by godly teachers of God's Word.

Yes, we grandparents should read our Bibles. But we want to read our Bibles rightly. What do I mean by that? Well, sometimes we read our Bibles as if the Bible itself is the source of our life. Is that how God wants us to approach his Word? Jesus dealt with people who read the Bible that way. He said, "You search the Scriptures because you think that in them you have eternal life; and it is they that bear witness about me" (John 5:39). They were thinking of the Bible as an end in itself—as a kind of rule book in which a person could make himself good enough for God. In treating the Bible this way, they were reading the right book but not reading it rightly. They were reading their Bibles, but missing Christ.

If we are going to read our Bibles in way that transforms the character of our lives, we must read the Bible in a Christ-centered way. We read our Bibles noticing our need for Christ. Seeing how he brings us to God. Seeing him. And, as we see Christ, the Spirit transforms us. Second Corinthians 3:18 explains, "And we all, with unveiled face, beholding the glory of the Lord, are being transformed into the same image from one degree of glory to another. For this comes from the Lord who is the Spirit." God's Word is a key tool that he uses in his ongoing work of shaping the character of our lives. But what are some of the other means of life transformation that we grandparents can and should embrace?

- *Prayer:* We ask the Spirit to have his way with us, transforming us to be more like Christ in daily life. We don't need to hesitate in making this request. He wants the Son to be honored, and he will graciously answer our request to accomplish his work of gradually changing us.
- *The examples of godly people in our lives:* Although, as the older generation, it is less common that we will have spiritual mentors in our lives, we still need the lives and examples of godly friends and leaders in our churches and the historic witness of the saints who have preceded us. "Whoever walks with the wise becomes wise" (Proverbs 13:20).
- *Responding in faith to life's difficulties and disappointments:* When I was a child, one of my elderly Sunday school teachers noted, "Hardships will make us either bitter or better." I remembered that. Having lived more years than the younger generations, we've had more opportunities to experience the pains and heartaches of living in this fallen world. Along life's journey, we have each experienced loss in various ways—loss of possessions, loss of health and abilities, loss of loved ones, and loss of hopes and dreams. In our pain, have we found hope and rest in Christ and the certainty of God's promises? Has the Spirit made us sweeter and stronger through our sufferings? Wherever we are, let us follow the apostle Paul in responding to hardship with hope: "[W]e rejoice in our sufferings, knowing that suffering produces

endurance, and endurance produces character, and character produces hope" (Romans 5:3–4).

I recently visited a nursing home at the invitation of one of the residents, a wheelchair-bound man who had been one of my Bible professors many years ago. He wanted to use our time together to discuss the Scriptures. I was impressed with this elderly man's desire to continue his quest to understand and apply God's Word, though he is now in his nineties. When I expressed how encouraging it was to see a man of his age still wanting to grow spiritually, he quoted 2 Peter 3:18. "But grow in the grace and knowledge of our Lord and Savior Jesus Christ." Then he asked me, "Did you hear Peter mention any retirement age from obeying this command?" Smiling, I replied, "No." We never retire from growing in the grace and knowledge of Jesus.

If we are going to leave a godly life-legacy for our grandchildren, we must continue to passionately pursue Christ and Christlikeness in daily life. Our lives will impact those of the coming generations. To some measure, our character, our priorities, and our perspectives on life and eternity will be reflected in them. May they see Christ in us!

Discussion Questions and Action Steps for Chapter 7

Discussion Questions:

1. Whose life impacted you the most as a young person? What was it about this person's life that gripped you?
2. At your funeral, what kinds of things do you hope your grandchildren will say about your impact on their lives? What will they say marked your life? What were you passionate about?

3. If you were to write out copies of your will for your grandchildren, what non-material things would you want to leave to them?

4. In Deuteronomy 4:9, before the directive for parents and grandparents to pass along to the coming generations the message of God's greatness and grace, there is this command: "Only take care, and keep your soul diligently." How does that command speak to you personally in your present situation?

Action Steps:

1. Write out two or three desires you have for your grandchildren. How do these reflect God's priorities as found in his Word? Do any necessary editing of your short list after careful reflection.

2. Plan a time for sharing your testimony with your grandchildren—the story of your own spiritual journey *to* Christ and *with* Christ.

3. Do you have some photo albums of your own children growing up? Plan a time to sit with your grandchildren and show them photos of their parents growing up, telling them stories and life lessons.

Conclusion

HAVE YOU EVER noticed that the apostle Paul sometimes reflected on his life as if he were running a race? He seems to have viewed his life as a sort of marathon with a defined destination in view—a finish line—and he didn't want to quit early! He didn't want to get off course. He wanted to run with purpose. His testimony in 1 Corinthians 9:26 was, "I do not run aimlessly." Day after day, year after year, he ran the race of his Christian life and carried out the ministry that the Lord had called him to while having the finish line in view. Toward the end of his race he told some of the church leaders he had discipled, "I do not account my life of any value nor as precious to myself, if only I may finish my course and the ministry that I received from the Lord Jesus, to testify to the gospel of the grace of God" (Acts 20:24).

You and I have a race to run, too. We are running the marathon of the Christian life. Along the way, we may be tempted to get off course with life's distractions or even to quit when we feel overcome with the weariness of living in a fallen world. But the author of Hebrews encourages us to persevere:

> Therefore, since we are surrounded by so great a cloud of witnesses, let us also lay aside every weight, and sin which clings so closely, and let us run with endurance the race that is set before us, looking to

Jesus, the founder and perfecter of our faith, who for the joy that was set before him endured the cross, despising the shame, and is seated at the right hand of the throne of God. Consider him who endured from sinners such hostility against himself, so that you may not grow weary or fainthearted. (Hebrews 12:1–3)

We are grandparents. That means, for most of us, we have fewer laps ahead of us than behind us. By God's grace, we want to finish our race well. We want to run our remaining laps with God-honoring perseverance and gospel-fueled joy. Our remaining laps include one of the most important ministries the Lord has entrusted to us—the ministry of grandparenting our precious grandchildren. We don't want to just mosey through our remaining laps in a self-focused, self-serving way. We want to reflect the grace the Lord has shown to us as we grandparent those young ones with loving, gracious intentionality.

My prayer is that this book will be used by the Holy Spirit as a catalyst in your life, encouraging you with a fresh view of the amazing calling the Lord has given us as grandparents to faithfully and intentionally draw our grandchildren's attention to the astonishing beauty and amazing grace of our Lord Jesus Christ "so that they should set their hope in God" (Psalm 78:4–7). Isn't that what you want more than anything else for your grandchildren? More importantly, isn't that what the Lord wants?

One day the time of our departure will come. We will finish our race (2 Timothy 4:6–8). By God's grace, may we hear those blessed words, the greatest commendation anyone could ever hear, "Well done, good and faithful servant" (Matthew 25:23). And, after our departure, our grandchildren who have been gripped by the grace of Jesus Christ will passionately tell their children and their grandchildren the wondrous deeds of the Lord in such a way that they, in turn, will tell generations yet unborn of the grace of the Lord Jesus Christ. Won't it be glorious to see our children and grandchildren and great-grandchildren alongside us in glory, praising our Savior with us? May we be faithful to our calling as gospel-centered grandparents!

"The grace of the Lord Jesus Christ and the love of God and the fellowship of the Holy Spirit be with you all"
(2 Corinthians 13:14).

Appendix

How to Be Right with God

MAYBE YOU'VE BEEN reading this book about intentionally pointing your grandchildren to Christ and his grace and have had the conviction growing in your own heart that maybe you have not experienced God's saving grace yourself. As important as it is to have a good relationship with your grandchildren, there is a relationship that is even more important—your relationship with the God who made you. The good news is that God wants to have a personal relationship with you, has accomplished all that is needed for that relationship, and even explains it all in his book, the Bible. We find these crucial truths in God's Word:

- *God has a created each of us for his purposes*: Each of us was born with a God-given "job description." The Bible clearly teaches that the Creator God designed you and me to reflect his glory with all that we are, with all that we have, and with all that we do in life (Isaiah 43:7). He created us to find our greatest joy in having a loving relationship with him—in seeking his smile and his honor in all things.

- *Not one of us, on our own, has done or can do what God created us for*: Even though God designed us to seek his glory in all that we do, we have selfishly sought our own honor instead. Even though God created us to find our greatest joy in him, we have ignored him and sought our happiness in our own possessions, power, and pleasure. Isaiah 53:6 reminds us of this painful diagnosis of our condition before God: "All we like sheep have gone astray; we have turned—every one—to his own way." Jesus Christ, God's Son, has been the single exception to this failure, and there has never been another sinless person since sin entered the human race at the time of our ancestors, Adam and Eve. "[A]ll have sinned and fall short of the glory of God" (Romans 3:23).

- *God has every right to condemn us to eternal punishment because of our willful rebellion against him*: Our rebellion against God—seeking our own glory instead of his and seeking our own happiness in the things of this world instead of in him as the Creator—is inexcusable. Our rebellion separates us from our loving Creator. This is not merely a matter of ignorance, as if we just didn't know. God has made his identity and power clear through what he has made in creation (Romans 1:18–20). No, our problem with God is more than a lack of knowledge. The shameful reality is that we're separated from God because we don't want him in our lives. Our refusal to honor God and find our joy in him is open rebellion against our Creator. The Bible calls that rebellion "sin," and sin rightfully earns God's condemnation: "The wages of sin is death" (Romans 6:23). And the ultimate death is to be eternally separated from God in a place of real, conscious torment known as hell or the lake of fire. The Bible gives this horrifying pronouncement about those who refuse to turn from their rebellion against God: "They will suffer the punishment of eternal destruction, away from the presence of the Lord and from the glory of his might" (2 Thessalonians 1:9).

- *We do not have the ability to fix our own terrible dilemma*: God's standard of acceptance is perfection—sinlessness. The Bible teaches that God is so pure, so holy, that he cannot tolerate sin in the slightest (Habakkuk 1:13). Yet we've all sinned. No amount of good intentions or religious devotion or benevolent deeds can compensate for or eradicate our sin and its guilt before the perfectly holy God who created us and holds us accountable. In fact, even our vain attempts to justify ourselves before God are offensive to him. He considers our feeble efforts to make ourselves presentable before his holy throne "like a polluted garment" (Isaiah 64:6). We cannot work our way out of our guilt and into God's good graces. Is our situation hopeless?

- *God himself has provided the only solution to our dreadful predicament*: The bad news is that we are undeniably, helplessly guilty before the holy God who made us and to whom we are accountable. The good news is that what we would not do and could not do, God did. The Bible tells us:

> For God has done what the law, weakened by the flesh, could not do. By sending his own Son in the likeness of sinful flesh and for sin, he condemned sin in the flesh, in order that

the righteous requirement of the law
might be fulfilled in us, who walk not
according to the flesh but according to
the Spirit. (Romans 8:3–4)

Jesus Christ, God's unique Son, came to Earth to
keep God's law perfectly. He did for us what we
should have done but could not do by ourselves.
He perfectly and consistently glorified God the
Father. Then Jesus also solved our horrifying sentence of guilt by taking on himself the wages of sin
that we had earned by our rebellion. He did this by
dying on the cross as a substitute for guilty sinners,
such as you and me. "For our sake he made him to
be sin who knew no sin, so that in him we might
become the righteousness of God" (2 Corinthians
5:21). As living proof that Jesus's sacrifice on the
cross for us satisfied God's holy requirements, God
raised Jesus from the dead. Jesus was "raised for
our justification" (Romans 4:25).

- *Christ's sacrifice on the cross opened the door for
us to have a right relationship with God*: God graciously calls us to repent of (turn from) our sin
and all of our attempts to justify ourselves in his
eyes. If we ever want to be right with God, we must
put all of our hope in Jesus Christ alone. The Bible
categorically declares, "[T]here is salvation in no
one else, for there is no other name under heaven
given among men by which we must be saved"
(Acts 4:12). God's Word also promises:

[I]f you confess with your mouth that
Jesus is Lord and believe in your heart
that God raised him from the dead,
you will be saved. For with the heart
one believes and is justified, and with

the mouth one confesses and is saved.
For the Scripture says, "Everyone
who believes in him will not be put
to shame." (Romans 10:9–11; Isaiah
28:16)

- *How will you respond?* Is God stirring your heart
  right now? Do you sense your sinfulness before
  the holy God who made you? Do you want to be
  right with him? Why don't you talk to God right
  now, asking him to forgive your sin and make
  you his child? Trust in Jesus Christ and what he
  accomplished on your behalf through his life,
  death, and resurrection. He will save you! He is
  gracious beyond your wildest imagination. "But to
  all who did receive him, who believed in his name,
  he gave the right to become children of God, who
  were born, not of blood nor of the will of the flesh
  nor of the will of man, but of God" (John 1:12–13).
  Isn't that amazing?

- *God wants you to grow in your relationship with
  him as you follow Jesus Christ*: If you have put your
  trust in Jesus Christ in order to have a right relationship with God, let me encourage you to follow
  through with some helpful steps. First, begin reading God's Word on a regular basis. That's how you
  get to know him better and understand how you
  can live for his glory. The Bible is a big book. Not
  sure where to start? Maybe start with the Gospel
  of Mark. That's the second book in the New
  Testament. Second, get into the wonderful habit of
  talking to God each day in prayer. You don't need
  fancy "religious" words. Just talk to him as your
  heavenly Father. And third, get plugged into a
  local church that is faithful in preaching, teaching,

and living out the Bible in a way that honors Jesus Christ. Tell some of the leaders of the church what God has been doing in your life and ask for their guidance. Welcome to the family!

An Annotated List
of Selected Resources
for Further Learning

THE NUMBER OF Christian books written on grandparenting is extremely small when compared to the number of books written about other family relationships, such as marriage or parenting. Some of those that have been published are more "anecdotal" in nature, telling stories and giving "tips" on grandparenting. The books that are devoted primarily to teaching biblical principles on grandparenting are few in number. Those that are gospel-centered are, to be frank, rare indeed. Here are a few resources that I have found helpful as a grandparent, pastor, and teacher of the Bible.

Harper, Cavin T. *Courageous Grandparenting: Unshakable Faith in a Broken World*. Colorado Springs, Colorado: The Christian Grandparenting Network, 2013.
Cavin Harper has been a pioneer of the Christian grandparenting movement, training a growing number of church leaders through The Christian Grandparenting Network.

Kimmel, Tim and Darcy Kimmel. *Extreme Grandparenting*. Carol Stream, Illinois: Tyndale House, 2007. The

Kimmels were some of the first to write a full-size book on biblical grandparenting.

Klumpenhower, Jack. *Show Them Jesus: Teaching the Gospel to Kids.* Greensboro, NC: New Growth Press, 2014. While not specifically written for grandparents, this book is rich with teaching on how to apply the gospel to children. It's worth your time.

Mulvihill, Josh. *Biblical Grandparenting.* Chaska, MN: atFamily, 2016. If you are a serious reader and want to know more of the Bible's teaching on grandparenting and the need for such teaching in our North American culture, start here.

Mulvihill, Josh, ed. *Equipping Grandparents.* Streamwood, IL: Legacy Coalition, 2016. Are you interested in starting a grandparenting ministry in your local church? This is a great resource, with articles contributed by some of the leaders in the burgeoning Christian grandparenting movement. Get this book for your pastors.

Penner, Lillian Ann. *Grandparenting with a Purpose.* Enumclaw, WA: Redemption Press, 2010. Lillian Penner is a national prayer coordinator for the Christian Grandparenting Network. This book has many helpful suggestions for growing in our ministry of praying for our grandchildren.

Some helpful websites:

Christian Grandparenting Network:
https://christiangrandparenting.net/

Legacy Coalition:
https://legacycoalition.com/

National Association for Grandparenting:
https://grandkidsmatter.org/

Endnotes

1. "Christ's Favor to Children," in *The Miscellaneous Writings of Matthew Henry* (London: Watts, 1811), 706.

2. See "Free Resources," *The Christian Grandparenting Network*. Accessed December 6, 2018. https://christiangrand parenting.net/product-category/free-resources/. Lillian Penner granted permission for adaptation.

3. See "How Close Do You Live to Your Grandchild?" *Statista* (March 2012). Accessed December 6, 2018. https://www.statista.com/statistics/241891/distance-between-us-grandparents-and-their-grandchildren/.

4. See Alejandra Cancino, "More Grandparents Raising Their Grandchildren," *PBS Newshour*, February 16, 2016. Accessed December 6, 2018. https://www.pbs.org/newshour/nation/more-grandparents-raising-their-grandchildren.

5. See Brandon Gaille, "23 Statistics on Grandparents Raising Grandchildren," *Brandon [Gaille]*, May 22, 2017. Accessed December 6, 2018. https://brandongaille.com/21-statistics-on-grandparents-raising-grandchildren/.